NICARAGUA

Jennifer Kott/Kristi Streiffert

MARSHALL CAVENDISH BENCHMARK

NEW YORK

PICTURE CREDITS
Cover photo: © Alamy: Robert Harding Picture Library Ltd.
alt.TYPE/Reuters: 1, 33, 43, 50, 69, 114 • Buddy Mays Photography: 44, 49, 55, 56, 82, 99 • Eye
Ubiquitous: 34 • Getty Images: 8, 59 • Horizon: 109 • Hulton-Deutsch: 28 • Hutchison Library: 6,
10, 30, 35, 45, 47, 108 • The Image Bank: 4, 15, 31 • Björn Klingwall: 11, 12, 90, 109, 121 • Heddy
Kuhl@javavino.com: 113 • Life File Photo Library: 9, 18, 22, 24, 27, 36, 38, 46, 48, 61, 62, 63, 64, 65, 66,
71, 72, 73, 74, 75, 76, 79, 80, 84, 87, 88, 89, 103, 104, 112 • Lonely Planet Images: 5, 60 • Keith Mundy:
3, 93 • Reuters Visnews: 7, 16, 41, 67, 100 • R. Ian Lloyd: 92 • Pietro Scòlazzi: 20, 52, 53, 120, 126
• David Simson: 105, 110, 111, 116, 118, 128 • Stockfood/Michael Cogliantry: 130 • Superstock, Inc.:
101 • Audrius Tomonis/www.banknotes.com: 135 • Travel Ink/David Forman: 106

PRECEDING PAGE
Performers in masks and costumes prepare for the start of the San Sebastián festival in the city of
Diriamba. The festival is considered one of the most colorful events in Nicaragua.

Marshall Cavendish Benchmark
99 White Plains Road
Tarrytown, NY 10591
Website: www.marshallcavendish.us

Originated and designed by Times Editions
An imprint of Marshall Cavendish International (Asia) Private Limited
A member of Times Publishing Limited

Library of Congress Cataloging-in-Publication Data
Kott, Jennifer, 1971-
   Nicaragua / by Jennifer Kott. – 2nd ed.
      p. cm. – (Cultures of the world)
   Summary: "Explores the geography, history, government, economy, people,
      and culture of Nicaragua" – Provided by publisher.
   Includes bibliographical references and index.
   ISBN 0-7614-1969-1
   1. Nicaragua – Juvenile literature. I. Title. II. Series: Cultures of the world (2nd ed.)
   F1523.2.K66 2005
   972.85 — dc22   2005009240

Printed in China

7 6 5 4 3 2 1

CONTENTS

A political wall mural.

Years of fighting have left their mark on this bullet-riddled wall.

INTRODUCTION

LOCATED LIKE A BULL'S-EYE in the middle of Central America, Nicaragua is a beautiful tropical land with breathtaking mountain ranges and exotic rain forests. It has a long history of partisan hostilities, poverty, repression, and foreign occupation. Despite its problems, however, the country has a strong tradition of family unity and the courage and optimism to build a better future. Nicaraguans have worked hard to reduce illiteracy, racial injustice, and infant mortality, and they are continuing with their struggle to improve living conditions.

Perhaps what makes Nicaragua such an interesting nation is its people's determination to enjoy life in spite of their troubles. With a rich tradition of poetry and a particular affinity for conversation, Nicaraguans are kind, generous, and insightful people. Although Nicaragua has hard-to-solve political problems and is the poorest of all the countries of Central America, today the hope of a better tomorrow looks bright.

GEOGRAPHY

PICTURE AN AREA about the size of the state of New York, covered with forests, lakes, mountains, and volcanoes. Imagine long coastlines looking out onto the Pacific Ocean and Caribbean Sea. This is how Nicaragua looks from an airplane flying over Central America. It is the largest country in the isthmus that lies between Mexico and South America, which is made up of seven countries, including Belize, Guatemala, Honduras, El Salvador, Costa Rica, and Panama.

To the north of Nicaragua lies Honduras, and to the south is Costa Rica. The western border is the Pacific Ocean, and to the east is the Caribbean Sea, which joins the Atlantic Ocean. In all, Nicaragua has about 560 miles (900 km) of coastline. At 49,998 square miles (129,494 square km), Nicaragua is a little smaller than Louisiana. Large areas of the country are uninhabited; most of its people are concentrated in the western region and in a few cities. The country's population per square mile is relatively thin compared to other Central American countries.

Left: **A volcano in Nicaragua's western volcanic area. Earthquakes and volcanic eruptions are frequent occurrences in Nicaragua.**

Opposite: **The active Santiago volcano at the Volcan Masaya National Park on the west coast. Rumors claim that during his reign, the dictator Anastasio Somoza García ordered the National Guard to drop political prisoners into Santiago's crater from a helicopter.**

THREE REGIONS

Nicaragua is divided into three geographic regions: the western Pacific lowlands, the central highlands, and the eastern Caribbean lowlands (also called the Mosquito Coast). Each region has features and weather characteristics that differentiate it from other parts of the country.

PACIFIC LOWLANDS Three out of four Nicaraguans live in the western part of the country between the Pacific coast and Lake Managua. Here, the land is good for crop cultivation because it has been enriched over the years by volcanic ash. Many of the people who live here work on farms, but Nicaragua's three biggest cities, León, Managua, and Granada are also in this region. The largest is Managua, the nation's capital.

CENTRAL HIGHLANDS East of Managua lies the area known as the central highlands. This mountainous area is covered with dense rain forest and receives an annual rainfall of between 70 and 100 inches (1,800 and 2,540 mm).

This is an inspiring, beautiful land of coffee plantations and cool, misty forests. In the northern mountains is a rich mining district called Nueva Segovia. Few people are willing to live in this humid place and take up the difficult work of mining the area's silver and gold.

MOSQUITO COAST Even wetter than the central highlands is the Mosquito Coast, which runs along the eastern third of the country. This region is the wettest area in Central America, with average annual rainfall ranging from 100 to 250 inches (2,540 to 6,350 mm). Much of the soil is gravel and sandy clay, with the only variation being a treeless, grassy plain called a savanna.

These Nicaraguans on the Mosquito Coast sell their farm produce from a makeshift roadside shack.

This area was named after the Miskito people, who have lived here for centuries. When the Spanish name, Costa Miskito, was translated into English, it became Mosquito Coast, possibly because the area was infested with mosquitoes. In addition to the Miskito, the other main groups who live here are the Rama and Sumo, who are natives of Nicaragua—and the Garífuna, who were originally from Africa. These groups have lived in this swamp-like region for many generations. Many build their houses on stilts for protection from floods and snakes.

Few Nicaraguans travel between the Pacific coast and the Mosquito Coast. Only a few roads link the two sides of the country, so travel is mostly by plane and boat.

Lake Nicaragua, believed to have been once part of the Pacific Ocean, was probably formed when volcanic activity raised the land around the lake, at the same time cutting it off from the ocean.

LAKES AND RIVERS

A network of waterways throughout Nicaragua play an important role in the country's system of transportation, commerce, and daily life. For example, the best farmland is near the lakes, rivers, and seas. Rivers mark the boundaries between Nicaragua and its neighbors Honduras and Costa Rica. City residents often take advantage of a sunny weekend by driving to one of the many resorts on the shores of Lake Nicaragua.

Nicaragua has two large lakes: Lake Managua and Lake Nicaragua. The larger of the two is Lake Nicaragua, also called by its more historical name Lake Cocibolca. Measuring 45 miles (72.4 km) wide and 110 miles (177 km) long, it has three volcanoes and over 300 islands, most of which are inhabited. Lake Nicaragua is Central America's largest lake, and the world's 10th largest freshwater lake. Perhaps the most remarkable feature is its unique inhabitants—freshwater sharks. Río Tipitapa connects this lake to Lake Managua, which covers 390 square miles (1,010 square km).

The Río Coco Oregovia forms part of the border with Honduras, and the Río San Juan forms part of the border with Costa Rica before emptying into the Caribbean Sea. Other rivers important to Nicaragua's transportation system include the Escondido and the Río Grande.

Ever since Christopher Columbus sailed along the coast of what is now Nicaragua in the 16th century, explorers had hoped to find a passage that would connect the Pacific Ocean on the west to the Atlantic Ocean on the east. While the Río San Juan does run nearly from coast to coast, it is not suitable for heavy traffic by freighters and other large vessels.

In the 19th century, Americans and Europeans studied a plan to build a canal to join the two oceans, providing ships with a fast and inexpensive route between the east and west coasts of the United States. The U.S. committee responsible for finding the best place to build the canal first chose Nicaragua, but disagreements with the Nicaraguan president resulted in Panama being selected as the site for the connecting waterway.

Main road in Tipitapa, a town located near Río Tipitapa.

The tranquil lakeside setting of Momotombo volcano belies the destructive force that lurks within.

VOLCANOES AND OTHER NATURAL HAZARDS

Volcanoes are largely responsible for the geographic makeup of Nicaragua. Many lakes and islands were formed by volcanic activity. Cities developed near the volcanoes because fertile farmland there attracted early settlers.

At least a dozen active volcanoes and many more dormant ones give the landscape a beautiful quality, but these peaks also pose a threat to Nicaraguans. Most of the population lives near active volcanoes. Thus, at any time, their homes and crops could be destroyed by an eruption or an earthquake caused by underground volcanic activity. The city of Managua still bears the scars of one such devastating earthquake that occurred just before Christmas in 1972. Managua is actually built on top of old volcanic rock that has been pressed together, not on solid rock.

Frequent earthquakes have caused destruction to Nicaragua throughout the country's history. The western part of the country lies along the Ring of Fire, a chain of volcanoes and fault lines that encircles the Pacific Ocean. It is called the Ring of Fire because of the high volume of volcanic activity there. Some of the volcanoes in Nicaragua that have erupted in the past two decades include Cerro Negro, Momotombo, San Cristóbal, Telica, and Concepción. Concepción and another volcano, Madera, make up Ometepe Island in Lake Nicaragua, on which at least eight small

MOUNTAIN IN MOTION

Cerro Negro exploded on April 10, 1992, and threw fire high into the sky. Car-sized boulders and scorching sand rained onto the surrounding villages and countryside. A cloud of ash darkened the sky above León and blanketed the city with a thick layer of dark gray powder.

The volcano, 15 miles (24 km) southwest of León, had erupted unexpectedly after lying dormant for 21 years. The initial blast injured at least 40 people and left two others dead. The volcano spewed sand and ash for almost two days, and nearby villages had to be evacuated. Then for 28 hours, the volcano was quiet. Suddenly, four days later, the 2,214-foot (675-m) volcano erupted again. Crops, homes, and livestock were destroyed and the damage stretched beyond the villages to León, leaving about 23,000 people homeless. It was the 16th time that the volcano had been active since it first erupted in 1867.

villages are built—proof that Nicaraguans have learned to coexist with the volcanoes that dominate the skyline.

Although living near the Ring of Fire can be dangerous, Nicaragua's turbulent government and economy have made it difficult to support research on volcanoes and earthquakes. In 1974 the United States donated seismic equipment to encourage the study of earthquakes and volcanoes, but they soon fell into disuse. Now, seismologists and volcanologists have set up stations in villages and cities located near volcanoes to monitor the earth's movements. The Nicaraguan Institute of Territorial Studies is also studying the volcanoes and their effects on the country.

Nicaragua's government is optimistic about using the country's abundant geothermal resources to reduce their need for imported oil. A geothermal plant near the Momotombo volcano, about 50 miles (81 km) from Managua, generates nonpolluting energy using the steam that rises from the depths of the volcano. There are plans to build more geothermal plants in Nicaragua in the near future.

Unfortunately, Nicaragua also suffers from other natural calamities that cause widespread destruction, such as drought, tsunamis, and hurricanes. Hurricane Mitch, which devastated Nicaragua and Honduras in October 1998, was one of the most deadly hurricane to hit the Western Hemisphere in the modern era. The hurricane killed more than 3,000 people and caused more than $1 billion in damages in Nicaragua, leaving thousands homeless and many of the country's roads destroyed.

Between 1990 and 2001, Nicaragua suffered three strong earthquakes and two major volcanic eruptions.

CLIMATE AND SEASONS

Managua, the capital, is located about 87 degrees west of the prime meridian, at about the same longitude as Memphis, Tennessee and lies about 12 degrees north of the equator. A line running east from Managua would pass about 1,025 miles (1,650 km) south of Miami.

As Nicaragua is located near the equator, it has a tropical climate—warm in the morning, hot and humid in the afternoon, and pleasant at night. In the mountainous regions of northwest Nicaragua, the higher altitude makes the average temperature a little cooler, especially at night. Also, the northern part of the country is a little less humid than the southern part. Even so, the weather in Nicaragua is hotter and more humid than what most North Americans are used to experiencing.

The climate in the eastern part of Nicaragua is always about the same— hot and wet. Few people live there because much of the land is covered with rain forest and jungle. It is the perfect home for monkeys, alligators, and snakes. Bananas, coconuts, persimmons, and other tropical fruit also thrive in this climate.

Snakes and monkeys thrive in the rain forests, where it is warm and humid.

14

In the more densely populated western low-lands, there are two seasons: the wet season from May to November and the dry season from December to April. During the wet season, it rains heavily almost every day, and there is little warning before a storm. The hottest, driest months of the year are March and April. For a few weeks in July and August, the rain stops again, the weather gets very hot, and everyone suffers from the heat.

The average temperature in the lowlands is about 86°F (30°C). The sun is blazing hot, and Nicaraguans often try to protect themselves from its damaging effects. Women sometimes carry umbrellas to provide some shade if they are out in the open for a long time. Men wear straw hats with strings that are tied into a knot under the chin to shade their eyes while working in the fields or walking outdoors.

Very few homes have air conditioning—in fact, most do not even have electric fans. In Managua, a few upper-class homes, offices, and restaurants have air conditioning, but most people just have to tolerate the heat. Despite the climate, young Nicaraguans faithfully followed fashion fads—even when it meant wearing *plásticos* (plast-EE-koh), or clothes made of plastic, a style that was popular in the discos in the mid-1980s.

Rich vegetation typical of the country's rain forests.

15

Government complex in Managua, the capital city beside Lake Managua.

MAJOR CITIES

MANAGUA With an estimated population of 1.1 million people, Managua is the largest city in Nicaragua. Nearly one-fourth of the population lives here. From the top of Loma de Tiscapa (Tiscapa Hill), the whole city is visible. The most beautiful part of this view is the Tiscapa Lagoon, a shallow pond that shimmers in the sun. The lagoon, which formed after rainwater filled a crater made by a volcanic eruption, is surrounded by lush green trees.

Managua became an important city in 1852 when two rival political factions, the Liberals and the Conservatives, settled their differences by choosing the sleepy town as the nation's capital. Before this decision, León and Granada were the two most important cities in Nicaragua. The Liberals dominated León and the Conservatives controlled Granada. The two groups fought many battles before agreeing to make Managua the capital.

The city has a drawback; since it is situated on a major fault line near a volcano, earthquakes occur frequently. During the Christmas 1972 earthquake, 10,000 people were killed and the city was destroyed. Recovery has been a long, slow process that may never be completed. Parts of Managua still lie in ruins, and subsequent earthquakes have hindered plans to rebuild the city.

The government has decided not to rebuild anything in the worst-hit areas. Instead, new development in Managua, just as in many cities in the United States, has been outside the city where new neighborhoods, shops, and restaurants are being built.

Over the past decade, a few modern shopping malls with department stores and movie theaters have sprung up in Managua, along with numerous modern supermarkets and American fast food restaurants.

GRANADA Nicaragua's oldest city, Granada, was founded in 1524 by Spanish explorer Francisco Hernández de Córdoba. Like Managua, it is also located on the shore of a lake and near a volcano. It is the country's second largest city and an important commercial area. Granada's volcano has left the area around the town fertile, and coffee and sugarcane are two important crops grown there.

Like all cities in Nicaragua, Granada has seen its share of fighting caused by political conflict, which has ravaged the country for years. Many factories and buildings have suffered heavy damage and are still being repaired. There are a hundred or so tiny islands east of Granada in Lake Nicaragua. These *isletas* (ees-LEH-tahs) are said to have been created when Granada's volcano erupted, blowing its lake-facing side into the water. The islands are linked by motorboat taxis, and wealthy Nicaraguans have built cottages there for weekend retreats.

LEÓN León was also founded by Hernández. In the Spanish colonial period, it was the capital of Nicaragua.

León had a huge cathedral built as a result of a mix-up in blueprints. The ruling Spanish government mistakenly sent to León the design for a cathedral in Lima, the capital of Peru, another Spanish colony. The blueprint for León's cathedral was, in turn, sent to Lima, which explains why that large city has such a tiny cathedral. Outside the city are beaches, resort towns, and a fertile agricultural area. Much of the dry, flat plain around the city is planted with cotton.

León and Granada, both within 50 miles (80.5 km) of Managua, are very important to the history of Nicaragua, but they seem more like large towns than cities. Both have populations of between 100,000 and 200,000 people, and neither have modern supermarkets or department stores similar to those found in Managua.

Sugarcane is an important crop as Nicaragua exports processed sugar.

NATURAL RESOURCES

Agriculture is an important part of life in Nicaragua. Almost half of the employed people work on farms. During the dry season, when crops are harvested, schools are closed so that children can help with the farm work.

Many crops—from beans and bananas to sugarcane and rice—grow well in Nicaraguan soil. Corn, coffee, cotton, tobacco, and cacao are the most important crops, while beans and rice are grown mainly for domestic consumption. The country's chief agricultural exports are coffee, beef, sugar, and seafood. Also important is gold. Other important minerals include silver, copper, tungsten, lead, and zinc.

Timber is another natural resource. Valuable mahogany, ebony, and rosewood trees grow in the highlands, and the northern Atlantic area is rich in pines. The once-thriving timber industry is slowly recovering from the effects of Hurricane Mitch in 1998 and from changes in forestry management that come from shifting government policies.

About 16 percent, or 8,000 square miles (20,720 square km), of the land is considered arable, or suitable for growing things. Of this land, roughly 1,000 square miles (2,590 square km) are actively cultivated. Another large portion of the land is used for grazing cattle.

SHARK!

Lake Nicaragua is the only freshwater lake in the world that is home to sharks. Stories of missing swimmers abound, but while people suspect the predatory inhabitants, no deaths due to shark attacks have been documented.

The lake was probably formed long ago when volcanic activity cut the area off from the Pacific Ocean. For many years it was believed that marine life became trapped in the lake while it still contained salt water. As the character of the lake gradually changed to fresh water, the saltwater fish adapted to living in fresh water and were able to reproduce. Another theory is that sharks traveled back and forth between the Atlantic Ocean and the lake. In 1966, after a decade of research that involved putting identification tags on sharks, American zoologist Thomas B. Thorson reported that bull sharks, a ferocious and versatile predatory species, enter the lake via the Río San Juan from the Atlantic Ocean, looking for food. The sharks, which can grow to 10 feet (3 m) and weigh up to 400 pounds (181.4 kg), can adapt to fresh water.

Another typically saltwater species found in the lake is the sawfish, which can weigh up to 1,000 pounds (453.6 kg). In the 1950s and 1960s, when the lake's population of these fish was much bigger, commercial fishermen netted thousands of sharks and sawfish. Since the 1990s, however, the population of both sharks and sawfish have declined and catching one of them today is rare.

FLORA AND FAUNA

Many varieties of plants and animals are indigenous to Nicaragua and other Central American countries. Some of the plants and trees, such as cedar, oak, and pine, are just as easily found in Nicaragua as in countries in the north. But because Nicaragua's climate varies from region to region, such tropical plants as tamarind and persimmon trees can also be found.

Many animal species found in North America also live in parts of Nicaragua. For example, deer, rattlesnakes, and coyotes are common in the highlands and in some sections of the western lowlands. As Nicaragua's climate is different than that in temperate countries, animals usually only seen in zoos inhabit areas of this tropical country, especially the jungles. These exotic animals include toucans, sloths, monkeys, jaguars, wild boars, and boa constrictors. Coral reefs are also found off the coasts.

HISTORY

THE HISTORY OF NICARAGUA goes back to the late Stone Age. Nicaragua has been an independent republic for less than 200 years.

Nicaraguans have been ruled by the Spanish, other Central American states, the U.S. Marines, local dictators, a socialist regime, and most recently, a democratically elected president and National Assembly. As a republic, the nation has survived nearly 30 years of near anarchy, followed by several decades of dictatorship and two civil wars.

THE FIRST PEOPLE

Anthropologists and archaeologists have found evidence that people have lived in Nicaragua from about 6,000 to 10,000 years ago.

The early people who settled in the west and center of the country were related to the Aztecs and Maya of Mexico. They probably found the fertile soils in the region suitable for growing food, and so settled in simple villages. Corn and beans were their main crops. One of the largest of these groups of people was the Nicarao, who inhabited much of the Pacific lowlands. Along the eastern coast, a group of ethnically different indigenous people hunted, fished, and practiced slash-and-burn agriculture. Their staple foods were root crops, such as cassava, plantains, and pineapples.

The indigenous people, such as the Nicarao, produced intricate works of art, especially pottery and gold jewelry. Religion and trading networks were important to their lives.

Above: **A Spanish galleon. In the 16th century, Spanish explorers sailed to the New World in ships like these.**

Opposite: **One of the many pre-Columbian statues in the town of Altagracia on Ometepe Island.**

Central plaza in Granada with fountain and bandstand.

SPANISH RULE

After Christopher Columbus traveled to Central America and reported to the king of Spain that great wealth could be found there, many Spanish explorers set out for the New World in search of riches. One such explorer was the conquistador, or conqueror, Gil González Dávila. In 1522 he became the first European to arrive in Nicaragua, but before he could form a settlement, the indigenous peoples chased him off the land.

One of Spain's earlier colonies was in Panama, where Pedro Arias de Ávila, or Pedrarias, became the ruler. He sent his lieutenant, Francisco Hernández de Córdoba, on a special mission to Nicaragua, and in 1523 Hernández landed in the country. He founded two cities, Granada and León, and went against Pedrarias' wishes by trying to make Nicaragua a separate Spanish province.

By Pedrarias' order, Hernández was beheaded, and Pedrarias became Nicaragua's governor from 1526 to 1531. He conquered the Nicaraguans just as he had conquered the indigenous people in Panama—by force. In fact, the Spaniards conquered large areas of Latin America, forcing its peoples to obey Spanish rules and customs, teaching them the Spanish version of world history, and replacing their religions with the Roman Catholic faith.

The leaders chosen to govern Nicaragua were often cruel to the indigenous groups. Indigenous people had to work on the Spaniards's farms rather than farming their own land. Being forced to give up their traditions made the natives resentful of the government. A large number of the original inhabitants who had survived warfare with the Spanish conquistadores were sent to Peru and other Spanish colonies as slaves

GOVERNING THE COLONIES

As the Spanish Empire grew, the king of Spain established a branch of the Spanish government, called the Supreme Council of the Indies, responsible for the colonies in Latin America. The highest office was that of viceroy. Other offices controlled every aspect of life in the colonies, from trade to religion and customs.

Central America was divided into three judicial areas called *audiencias* (aw-dee-EN-see-ahs). Nicaragua was originally part of the *audiencia* of Panama, but in 1544 the country came under the authority of the audiencia of Guatemala. The chief executive in each *audiencia* was called the governor, but he served the roles of president, governor, and head of the military. The king of Spain appointed the governors. The governor appointed *corregidores* (koh-reh-he-DO-res) or magistrates, who ruled smaller towns inhabited mostly by indigenous people.

to work in mines. Mestizos, or people of mixed indigenous and Spanish descent, tried to avoid forced labor by adopting Spanish customs and denouncing their aboriginal heritage.

Between 1519 and 1650 an estimated two-thirds of all indigenous people living in Central America lost their lives as a result of warfare, disease, and slavery. Those who survived were forced off their land because the conquistadores wanted to build cities there.

During the 1660s, the Spanish introduced a system of local government into Nicaragua. Property owners selected the members of a town council, and the position of council member was passed down from father to son. Usually these offices were held by residents of Spanish ancestry who were born in the colonies.

People of Spanish ancestry were a privileged class in Nicaragua at the time. They controlled much of the trade and had the most political power. Spanish people lived pretty much as they pleased, while the indigenous people were treated harshly.

In the 17th century natural disasters, trade restrictions imposed by Spain, and the local government's neglect of agricultural production caused much economic hardship among the Nicaraguans.

By the early 19th century, people across Central America had become unhappy with Spain's rule, which they saw as unjust. In 1821 Nicaragua and the rest of Central America declared their independence.

The indigenous peoples' cultural identity also suffered under the Spanish, but one aspect of it still remains today: the word Nicaragua comes from Nicarao, the name of the chief of the main aboriginal nation and is thought to mean "here near the lake," referring to Lake Nicaragua.

Single-cropping—such as in the picture above —was not prevalent in newly independent Nicaragua, since farmers grew what they needed to consume and only sufficient beyond that for cash to buy what they could not grow or make.

INDEPENDENCE

After Nicaragua declared its independence from Spain in 1821, it became part of the Mexican Empire. In 1823 Nicaragua left the empire to join the United Provinces of Central America, an organization of former Spanish colonies ruled by a central government in Guatemala City. Problems arose when Nicaraguan officials became unhappy with Guatemala's attempts at centralizing power. One major disagreement was over the building of a canal through Nicaragua. Nicaraguans saw the proposed canal as a way to increase the country's economic activity, but the central government decided it would take business away from ports in Guatemala. Eventually Nicaraguan officials decided the central government was too far away to understand their needs. In 1838 Nicaragua left the United Provinces and became an independent republic.

TUSSLE FOR THE EAST

In the late 17th century the Caribbean lowlands came under British influence. The British formed an alliance with one of the local aboriginal groups, the Miskito. The Miskito people later intermarried with slaves who had escaped from British plantations in the Caribbean. Between 1740 and 1786, the Mosquito Coast was a British dependency, and a tussle ensued between Spain and Britain for control of the region.

By the mid-1800s Nicaragua had become a focal point for the United States and Britain who were considering the creation of a passage across the isthmus to connect the Atlantic and Pacific oceans. Britain had consolidated its influence in the east with the departure of the Spanish, and was eager to develop any possible riches inside Nicaragua. Fearing a British takeover, Nicaragua turned to the United States for protection. But it was only during the presidency of José Santos Zelaya that the Mosquito Coast came under Nicaraguan jurisdiction.

THE TURNING POINT

In the 18th century two conflicting groups in Nicaragua had been formed. They differed on how the country should be run. In many ways, the two groups had similar goals, but they each had a different plan on how to achieve those goals. The group based in León became known as the Liberal party; the other group, the Conservative party, governed Granada. The Liberals favored political liberty, while the Conservatives favored political order and the ideas of the colonial past. This led to constant conflicts between the two groups that continues even today.

William Walker an American adventurer, was briefly president of Nicaragua in 1856.

An American adventurer, William Walker (1824–60), went to Nicaragua at the request of government officials in León. He was supposed to help them defeat Granada in a battle over which party would control the country. But after a bloody battle, Walker made himself president in 1856. For a year he ruled the country as an oppressive tyrant. Despite opposition from local leaders, he sold or gave land to U.S. companies, declared English the official language, and legalized slavery. He also tried to make Nicaragua part of the United States.

Nicaragua's two warring parties joined forces and recruited many peasants to help fight Walker. The people of Nicaragua succeeded in overthrowing Walker and forced him to leave the country.

Once the two partisan groups had stopped fighting among themselves, they were able to form a centralized government. However, from 1857 to 1893 almost all the presidents were conservatives. They passed laws that made it harder for peasants to own land, essentially taking away the farmers' livelihood.

At the beginning of the 19th century, land was wealth, and most Nicaraguans owned at least some land. By 1900, however, distinct class boundaries had formed, dividing poor peasant farmers from the wealthy landowners for whom they worked.

The actions of Zelaya, who became president in 1893, set off a chain of events that led to the United States' posting its Marines in Nicaragua.

UNITED STATES INVOLVEMENT

Around this time, the matter of building a canal to connect the two oceans once again became a relevant issue, leading to the start of uneasy relations with the United States. Zelaya, the liberal president who took office in 1893, refused to grant the United States unrestricted rights to build the canal. Many Nicaraguans, especially conservatives, opposed Zelaya, a harsh dictator.

The United States encouraged the conservative opposition to revolt against Zelaya. When two U.S. citizens who participated in the revolt were executed by Zelaya's officers, the United States decided it was time to take direct action. Four hundred U.S. Marines were sent in to preserve order. Stationed in Bluefields on the Mosquito Coast, the Marines tried to block a liberal victory. When Zelaya resigned in 1909, another liberal, José Madriz, took his place. The United States also refused to recognize Madriz. The civil war in Nicaragua continued for several more months until conservative president Adolfo Díaz took office in 1911.

A brief period of relative calm followed. But then Díaz made an agreement that turned over control of the country's finances to the United States as a condition for a loan from U.S. banks. The contract put the United States in charge of Nicaragua's finances until 1925, when the debt was paid off.

Soon the Marines were back, this time to deal with the forces that opposed U.S. control. In 1916 a treaty was ratified to give the United States exclusive rights to build a canal and to establish naval bases. Although the United States later decided to build the canal in Panama, the naval bases were built in Nicaragua. The U.S. Marines occupied Nicaragua almost continuously until 1933, protecting U.S. interests and supervising elections.

Eventually, the opposition rallied together under General Augusto César Sandino, who led

General Augusto César Sandino. Sandinistas took their name from Sandino.

the rebels from 1927 to 1933. These rebels named themselves Sandinistas after their leader and adopted guerrilla tactics, with small groups hiding in the mountains and periodically ambushing to attack the U.S. Marines.

27

President Anastasio Somoza García, head of the National Guard and the first of the ruling Somozas.

The Sandinistas knew they were greatly outnumbered by the U.S. Marines, but they fought anyway. General Sandino's motto was "Free homeland or death," and he often said, "It's better to die a rebel than to live as a slave."

Finally the United States decided to compromise. Instead of trying to impose democracy, it agreed to support any Nicaraguan leader who could promise peace in Nicaragua and friendship with the United States. In the 1932 election, the last supervised by the United States, a former rebel named Juan Bautista Sacasa became president.

The U.S. Marines trained a new Nicaraguan army to help the president keep order. The handpicked head of this National Guard was a former used-car dealer and health inspector, Anastasio Somoza García.

In 1934 after the U.S. Marines left Nicaragua, President Sacasa and General Sandino signed a peace treaty to end the fighting. However, Sandino also insisted the National Guard be dissolved. This led General Somoza to go behind the president's back and order the Guard to kill Sandino. The Guard also murdered more than 300 of Sandino's supporters. When President Sacasa tried to take away General Somoza's control over the Guard, he discovered that General Somoza was much too powerful. In 1936 General Somoza forced President Sacasa (who was his uncle) to resign, and by the following year, the general was president of Nicaragua.

THE SOMOZA DYNASTY

For the next 42 years (1937–79), the Somoza family ruled the country. President Somoza, who was called Tacho by his friends and family, was eager to cooperate with the United States. He had its support because he was not a Communist and was powerful enough to prevent rebels from causing another war. Under his rule, the Nicaraguan government became stable enough for U.S. corporations to start investing money in business prospects there. The economy expanded, but average Nicaraguans did not see the effects of this improvement.

Somoza had absolute power over the country's activities and used it to his personal advantage. When people tried to interfere with Somoza's authority, he had the National Guard threaten or kill them. He filled the Constituent Assembly with his supporters. The Assembly not only gave the president more powers, but in 1938 it also elected him for another eight-year term as president. In the 1940s the United States persuaded Somoza not to run for another term. Somoza then appointed a family friend to the presidency. In 1950 Somoza again assumed the presidency, but in 1956 at a ball in his honor, a poet, Rigoberto López Pérez, shot him dead in an attempt to end the dictatorship.

Somoza's eldest son Luis took over. During his five years in office, Luis tried to change the way the country was run. But in 1963 he was too ill to run for reelection. Instead, a close Somoza associate was elected president. In 1967 Luis died and his younger brother, Anastasio Somoza Debayle, won the elections that year. Somoza Debayle took over the country and ruled by his father's methods. Within a few years as president and head of the National Guard, he had increased his family's wealth to an estimated $900 million. The Somoza family owned one-fifth of the country's land, several sugar mills, factories, an airline, and several banks.

Anastasio Somoza Debayle, nick-named Tachito, objected to being called a dictator. He argued that as he allowed the newspaper La Prensa *to be published, he could not be a dictator. During the Somoza dynasty, however, less than half the population could read and a newspaper that criticizes the government is not much of a threat as long as the majority of the governed cannot read.*

Sandinista guards taking a break by a lake. Most of them were drafted into the army at the age of 17. Because of their extreme youth, people called them *los muchachos* (los moo-CHAH-chohs), or the kids.

CIVIL WAR AND REVOLUTION

By this time, a distinct upper class had developed that included friends and supporters of the Somozas, corporate leaders who profited from Somoza Debayle's unethical economic regime, and a few successful independent business owners. The rest of the population was mostly poor, and they were becoming more aware of Somoza Debayle's corruption. Bands of guerrilla rebels began to form. In the early 1960s the Sandinista National Liberation Front (FSLN) was founded, taking its name and some of its ideas from the rebels who fought under General Sandino in the 1920s. The FSLN members wanted Somoza Debayle out of office. They wanted to form a new government that would teach people to read and write, improve health care, provide food and housing, and give political power to workers and peasants. It was dangerous to be known as a Sandinista because the National Guard imprisoned or killed people whom they believed were associated with the FSLN.

Two events brought Somoza Debayle's abuse of power out into the open. First, in 1972 Somoza Debayle and his National Guard were accused of taking advantage of the terrible earthquake that destroyed Managua. Humanitarian aid poured in from all over the world, but very little of it actually made it into the hands of the people. Supplies, food, blankets, and medicines were allegedly confiscated by Somoza Debayle and his

Wall painting in Managua spawned by the political upheaval of the time.

officers and resold for their own profit. (Somoza Debayle later wrote a book called *Nicaragua Betrayed*, in which he explained his side of the story. He denied all the accusations of corruption following the earthquake.)

As more people found out about Somoza Debayle's abuse of power, the FSLN gained popularity, even among the middle class and businesspeople. In 1974 after the FSLN kidnapped a few government officials, some of whom were Somoza Debayle's relatives, the National Guard launched a violent attack on the FSLN. Many FSLN members were killed, including one of its founders, José Carlos Fonseca Amador.

When the second event, the assassination of newspaper editor Pedro Joaquín Chamorro, occurred in January 1978, the public was outraged. Nicaraguans loved Chamorro because he stood up to Somoza Debayle and printed articles in his newspaper, *La Prensa*, describing Somoza Debayle's corruption. Many people believed that the dictator had ordered Chamorro's murder. Thousands of demonstrators showed up at Chamorro's funeral.

In August 1978 the FSLN held the national palace hostage for two days. Although the crisis was eventually resolved, the National Guard responded by killing many civilians. The FSLN, in turn, captured many cities. Neighboring countries urged Somoza Debayle to resign. In July 1979 Somoza Debayle announced his resignation and fled the country. Up to 50,000 Nicaraguans are believed to have died in the conflict to unseat him.

THE CONTRA WAR

The Sandinistas ruled Nicaragua from 1979 to 1990. They tried to help the poor and improve the economy, but after a brief period of improvement, a new civil war began to take its toll on the economy and hamper the Sandinistas' efforts at social reform.

By the early 1980s a new group of rebels had formed. They were called counter-revolutionaries (or Contras) because they had grown disillusioned with the revolution and opposed the changes the Sandinistas were trying to make. Some contras were former National Guard members who set up military bases in neighboring Costa Rica and Honduras, in order to conduct armed raids into Nicaraguan territory.

In 1981 the United States accused the Nicaraguan government of supplying weapons to rebels in other Central American countries, when in reality, it was the Contras who were training with Honduran soldiers. The U.S. government feared that the Sandinistas were Communists who would allow the Soviet Union to set up military bases in Nicaragua; the Sandinistas received money and military aid in the form of tanks, fighter aircraft, and helicopter gunships from the Soviet Union and Cuba, another Communist country. Since U.S. officials perceived this as a threat to U.S. freedom and democracy, U.S. president Ronald Reagan authorized military aid to the Contras, and in 1985 declared a trade embargo on Nicaragua. This took place despite a 1982 legislation prohibiting the United States from supplying the Contras with arms to overthrow the Sandinista government.

The Contra war lasted until 1990, when a new president was elected. The winning campaign of Violeta de Barrios Chamorro, the first female president and widow of Pedro Chamorro, was endorsed by the United States because she planned to establish democracy in Nicaragua and introduce a free market economy. Although her years as president were marked by continued political struggles and economic problems, Chamorro initiated the creation of democratic institutions, worked toward national reconciliation, stabilized the economy, and reduced human rights violations. Doña Violeta, as Nicaraguans call her, became a beloved national figure.

CONTINUING TRANSITIONS

In 1996 Nicaraguans elected a new president, former Managua mayor Arnoldo Alemán, and celebrated as power was peacefully transferred from one democratically elected president to another. Some important programs were initiated during Alemán's years as president. But the collapse of coffee prices and the devastation caused by Hurricane Mitch slowed the progress. In 2003 the credibility of the presidency was damaged when Alemán was convicted of embezzlement and sentenced to 20 years' imprisonment.

In 2001 Alemán's former vice-president, Enrique Bolaños, was elected president. Bolaños, the candidate for the ruling Liberal Constitutionalist Party (PLC), received 56 percent of the vote as compared to 42 percent for Daniel Ortega, leader of the FSLN. However in 2003, Bolaños was forced to leave the PLC over his prosecution of Alemán.

Bolaños promised to address poverty, unemployment, and corruption and also to seek relief from the country's burden of international debt. His goal of lowering the national debt was met in 2004 when the World Bank forgave 80 percent of the country's debt. Later that year Russia also agreed to forgive Nicaragua's debt, which dated back to the Soviet era.

In August 2002 former president Arnoldo Alemán (above center) was charged with corruption. As head of the National Assembly, he received immunity from prosecution. But in November that year, the National Assembly voted to strip him of his position and immunity. Alemán was found guilty of money laundering, fraud, embezzlement, and electoral crimes in December 2003.

GOVERNMENT

NICARAGUA HAS SURVIVED dictatorships and a socialist-style government and is now working at strengthening a young democracy. Historically, transitions from one government to the next have never been peaceful in Nicaragua, but other than some initial armed rivalry, Chamorro's 1990 victory over former president Ortega marked the first time one political party peacefully transferred power to another. Although the armed conflicts have faded into the past, various groups are still trying to gain control of the country, making it hard for the government to concentrate on governing.

Above: **A government-organized May Day rally in Managua, in which workers celebrate the progress made since the country's independence.**

Opposite: **The National Assembly building on Bolivar Avenue in Managua.**

THE RIGHTS OF THE PEOPLE

When Nicaragua belonged to the United Provinces of Central America, its people lived under the region's constitution, approved in 1824. Upon nationhood in 1838, Nicaragua drew up a new constitution. All of these constitutions were written by liberals, so they guarded against tyranny and protected the freedom of the people. Each branch of government had defined areas of responsibility so no one branch had too much power.

Between 1838 and 1974 Nicaragua had 10 different constitutions. The latest, adopted in 1987, guards against absolute governmental power; protects freedom of speech, the press, and religion; and guarantees the right to own land. In 1995 the constitution was amended to reduce the presidential term to five years, rule out consecutive reelection, and bar relatives of serving presidents from standing for elections. The constitution was again amended in 2000 and in 2005, amid controversy, as the amendments shifted the balance of power from the president to the legislature.

KEY POLITICAL PLAYERS

FSLN The Frente Sandinista Liberación Nacional (Sandinista National Liberation Front) began as a small group of students who opposed Anastasio Somoza Debayle's oppressive rule. One of their leaders, José Carlos Fonseca Amador (*left*), urged the group to take up arms in revolt against Somoza Debayle's government. The FSLN became an underground movement that involved many young people who were willing to risk their lives to free their country from Somoza Debayle's grip.

Taking inspiration from Fidel Castro's revolution in Cuba, the FSLN assigned bands of guerrilla fighters to live in the mountains and carry out surprise attacks on the National Guard. After nearly falling apart several times, the FSLN finally developed into a revolutionary army capable of overthrowing Somoza Debayle. When FSLN succeeded, they selected people from within their ranks, together with other anti-Somoza organizations, to form a ruling junta (political faction). In 1984 the Sandinista party won the presidential election.

CONTRAS The Contras were rebels who opposed the revolutionary government (the Sandinistas). They include Somocistas, people who profited from the Somoza family's abuse of power and feared revenge by the new government. When Somoza Debayle's regime fell, many Somocistas fled the country, although the Sandinistas outlawed the death penalty and pardoned many of Somoza Debayle's collaborators.

Many business and political leaders were glad to see Somoza Debayle overthrown but did not fully agree with the Sandinistas' idea to redistribute the country's wealth. Some of them joined the FSLN to try to influence its policies, but when they realized the Sandinistas intended to carry out their original plans, they resigned from their government positions and helped to organize the Contras. One of these people was Violeta Chamorro, the only female member of the original five-member ruling junta selected by the Sandinistas. She left her position in the junta only nine months after being appointed to it. The largest Contra group was the Nicaraguan Democratic Force (FDN). Of its 48 commanders, 46 were former members of Somoza Debayle's National Guard. Their bases were mostly along the northern part of Nicaragua's border with Honduras. The other anti-Sandinista groups in the south did not join the FDN at first because of its link to the National Guard.

PLC The Partido Liberal Constitucionalista (Liberal Constitutionalist Party) rose in significance after Arnoldo Alemán became its leader in the early 1990s. A populist right-wing party, it was formed from the union of several smaller liberal parties that had broken off from former dictator Anastasio Somoza Debayle's National Liberal Party (PLN). Under Alemán, the PLC had joined with the UNO to oppose Sandinista control of the government. In 1997 Alemán won the presidency under the PLC banner. Current president Enrique Bolaños was also a PLC member until his anti-corruption campaign resulted in Alemán being jailed for embezzlement. Bolaños then lost support with the PLC and has now started his own political organization.

UNO The Unión Nacional Opositora (National Opposition Union) was a 14-party coalition of anti-Sandinista organizations. It backed Chamorro in the 1990 election, but the coalition suffered from internal divisions. In 1993, after accusations of corruption within the government, the UNO severed its ties with Chamorro and boycotted the National Assembly, leaving the Sandinistas in the majority.

UNITED STATES The United States feared that the Sandinistas were communists and would allow the Soviet Union to set up military bases in Nicaragua. The U.S. government opposed the Sandinistas and aided the contras to protect U.S. interests. Then-president Ronald Reagan sent the Contras weapons, money, and soldiers.

In 1984 Reagan charged the Sandinistas with setting up a communist dictatorship, and in 1985 he imposed a trade embargo against Nicaragua after Congress voted against his $14 million Contra-aid plan. Before the trade embargo, the United States was Nicaragua's chief trading partner. A year later, the Reagan administration was accused of diverting profits from secret arms sales to Iran to the Contras, even after Congress had prohibited any more military aid to the rebels. Further investigation into the Iran-Contra scandal concluded with an official report that members of Reagan's administration had acted illegally.

The U.S. Central Intelligence Agency (CIA) also helped the Contras. The CIA participated in the bombing of Managua Airport and helped blow up oil pipelines in several ports. It also directed an operation to place explosive mines in the harbor at Corinto, preventing ships carrying supplies from reaching land. In 1986 the World Court, the judicial arm of the United Nations, ruled that the United States was at fault for "training, arming, equipping, financing, and supplying the Contra forces." However, the World Court has no authority to enforce its decisions.

Sandinista revolutionary statue in Managua.

THE SANDINISTAS' SOCIALIST REGIME

SOCIALISM In a socialist regime, the national government is made up of a multimember directorate, but there is no concrete system of checks and balances. Typically, the government has complete control over the country's economy. The military plays a very important role because it enforces the policies made by the governing body. Traditional socialism basically focuses on equality. Socialists object to personal ownership of property, because they believe that a country's wealth should be equally earned and shared by everyone.

The Sandinista ideology followed socialism to some extent, but the Sandinistas always asserted that their revolutionary plan was specifically tailored to Nicaraguan needs. They wanted to bring about equality and national prosperity and hoped to narrow the enormous gap between the rich and poor. They confiscated property owned by wealthy Somoza supporters and turned it into state-run farming collectives, but two out of three farms remained privately owned.

WHO WAS IN CHARGE? From 1979 to 1984 the ruling body of the Sandinista government was a five-person junta selected from the FSLN and other groups that opposed Somoza Debayle. One of its members was Violeta Chamorro. During the first year, however, Chamorro and another member disagreed with the Sandinistas' new policies, so they left the government and formed opposition parties. Then, in a free election, Ortega was elected president of the Sandinista government. Some

WHERE THE SANDINISTAS FAILED

The Sandinistas wanted to unite the historically isolated eastern coast with the rest of the country, but in their attempt, they made mistakes. The Sandinistas saw the Miskito people as backward and needing to participate in the workforce. The Miskitos wanted recognition of their land rights and traditional use of the land. They also wanted self-government. But the Sandinistas thought they wanted independence. The Sandinista government also suspected the Miskitos of being Contras—some did support the Contras—and killed or imprisoned a number of suspected Contra supporters. To reduce the possibility of Contra influence on the Miskitos, the government uprooted entire Miskito communities from areas near the fighting and moved them to "safer" places inland.

The Sandinista government also had the habit of unfairly arresting and jailing people it believed to be supporting the Contras, including politicians and union leaders. Critics of the government cited its violation of religious freedom and the right to free speech. For example, executive orders repeatedly shut down the newspaper *La Prensa* because it published antigovernment opinions. Also, in 1985, the government forced 10 foreign priests to leave Nicaragua because they gave antigovernment sermons. The military draft was another highly criticized Sandinista action.

political groups say that the 1984 election was one of the fairest in Central American history, but others said it was unfair because opposition parties were not given enough freedom to campaign, so they had no real chance of winning. In addition to controlling the presidency and the National Assembly, the Sandinistas established a Council of State, a coalition of representatives from various political parties, labor unions, and business associations. The council acted as an advisory board to the lawmakers.

POLICIES, GOALS, AND IDEALS In their first few years in power, the Sandinistas' main goals were to raise the standard of living and to make everyone more equal by redistributing the country's wealth. For the previous four decades, most of the land, industries, and money had belonged to the Somozas and their friends. Immediately after taking office, the Sandinistas began giving the land to peasants so that they could grow enough food for their families. The next step was the nationalization of private industries. The economy took a slight upward turn when the Sandinistas began controlling agricultural exports, banking and finance, insurance, and mining. Businesses and farms owned by private citizens not affiliated with Somoza Debayle were allowed to continue normal operations.

The assassination of newspaper editor Pedro Joaquín Chamorro gave rise to much public outrage, which eventually led to the downfall of the Somoza regime.

RETURN TO DEMOCRACY

Since 1984 Nicaragua has held four presidential elections. In 1990 Chamorro defeated the incumbent Ortega to become the president. Before she decided to run for president, she was best known as the widow of Pedro Joaquín Chamorro, the editor of the antigovernment *La Prensa* newspaper, who was assassinated during Somoza Debayle's regime.

Former mayor of Managua, Alemán, won the 1996 elections; his vice-president, Bolaños, was subsequently elected president in 2001. The next presidential election will be held in late 2006.

The Nicaraguan government consists of three branches: the executive, legislative, and judicial.

THE PRESIDENT In Nicaragua, the president is both chief of state and head of the government. Nicaraguans vote directly to elect the president for a five-year term, and anyone over 16 can vote. The president stays in office for one term only, as the constitution forbids anyone from holding office for consecutive terms. In 2005 a controversial amendment to the constitution allowed the president to be removed from office for criminal offences. However, this clause will take effect only after the term of the current president, Bolaños, ends in late 2006.

THE NATIONAL ASSEMBLY Nicaragua is divided into 15 departments (much like provinces) and two autonomous regions. Based on their population, the departments and regions get a certain number of representatives in the National Assembly, which is the legislative branch of the government. The National Assembly is unicameral as it does not have two separate houses of representatives. It is made up of 90 elected representatives, the country's former president, and the runner-up in the presidential election, for a total of 92 representatives.

Under the 1995 constitutional amendment, the National Assembly received more power than the 1987 constitution had permitted. For instance, it now has greater control over the budget, taxation, and international accords. The National Assembly has the power to override a presidential veto with

Violeta Chamorro, the first woman president of Nicaragua and Central America.

a simple majority, and it also has the right to nominate candidates for top ministerial positions. The 2000 and 2005 constitutional amendments also gave the National Assembly more powers, which its supporters claim will balance out the president's role. Those who disagree say that the power of government now rests with the two largest political parties in the country, which also control most of the seats in the National Assembly—the PLC and the FSLN.

THE JUDICIARY The judicial branch consists of several court districts spread out over the country, with each district representing several departments. The Supreme Court is in Managua, and the next highest courts are five Chambers of Second Instance, located in León, Granada, Masaya, Matagalpa, and Bluefields. The National Assembly elects the 16 Supreme Court judges to five-year terms, based on a list of candidates submitted by the president. Judges of the lower courts are appointed by the Supreme Court.

THE POLITICAL STRUGGLE CONTINUES

One year into her presidency, Violeta Chamorro's approval rating stood at around 77 percent. But by the time she left office, her approval rating had fallen to less than 30 percent. Since then, her approval rating has steadily risen. In 2005 over 77 percent of people polled regarded Chamorro favorably. But she has steadfastly refused to get involved in politics again.

Before Chamorro took office, there were frequent battles between the Contras and Sandinistas. Both parties were reluctant to lay down arms. Just days before Chamorro's inauguration, the outgoing Sandinista government, the Contra rebels, and Chamorro's representatives signed agreements to establish an immediate ceasefire. The Contras agreed to begin surrendering all weapons to international authorities on April 25, 1990, and to complete demobilization by June 10, 1990.

About 20,000 Contras and their families returned from Honduras, turned their weapons over to the authorities, and went back to their homes in Nicaragua. Not all accepted the ceasefire. In 1990 estimates of the still-armed Contras varied between 700 and 1,000; later more took up arms again. These rebels were called *recontras* (ray-KOHN-trah). Former members of the Sandinista army, called *recompas* (ray-KOHM-pah), fought the Chamorro administration as well as the *recontras*.

Frequent outbreaks of violence troubled the nation. In July 1993 a group of about 150 *recontra* rebels captured the northern city of Estelí. The ensuing battle left 45 people dead. Two months later, *recontras* took 38 government officials hostage and demanded the dismissal of Chamorro's head of the army and her chief of staff in exchange for the hostages' release. The next day, the *recompas* took 34 hostages at the UNO headquarters in Managua, including Vice President Virgilio Godoy Reyes. They demanded the release of the other hostages and monetary compensation from the United States. The situation was resolved within a week.

Many of the Chamorro administration's actions prompted Nicaraguans and outsiders alike to ask, "Who is really ruling Nicaragua?" When Ortega was voted out of office, the FSLN retained enough seats in the National Assembly to prevent constitutional change. The UNO felt that Chamorro was weak and incapable of standing up to the Sandinistas. Thus in 1993, the UNO officially parted ways with Chamorro. Many had thought that when the Sandinistas were defeated by President Chamorro, their influence would fade away. But even today, the Sandinistas still maintain strong political power.

Since Chamorro, Nicaragua has had two more democratically-elected presidents, Alemán and Bolaños, yet Nicaragua's poor still look up to FSLN leaders, because the Sandinistas continue to express their commitment to the poor by advocating the redistribution of income. The FSLN won many community elections in 2004 and their leader, Ortega, has remained an active political force. The FSLN has held about 40 percent of the vote in national elections since it lost control of the presidency in 1990.

The power struggle between the executive and legislative branches of the government has also affected the stability of the country. In 2005 the FSLN and the PLC, the two parties with the most seats in the National Assembly, passed a legislation to amend the constitution. One amendment transferred the power to appoint cabinet ministers from the president to the National Assembly.

Nicaragua has also been struggling to overcome a deep-rooted system of political corruption. When President Bolaños took office he promised to attack corruption by holding officials accountable. Foreign investors and foreign aid organizations hoped for success because they wanted less of their money to be sidetracked to dishonest government officials. But corruption, and the greed that underlies it, is hard to overcome, and it remains to be seen if Bolaños' efforts will be effective.

Enrique Bolaños was elected president of Nicaragua in 2001.

ECONOMY

NEW BUSINESSES, shops, restaurants, and super-markets have sprung up all over Managua, the capital city, since a free market economy returned to Nicaragua. Gone are the days of state-run farms and government-controlled banks. Nicaragua now sports the look of an up-and-coming commercial enterprise; but looks can be deceiving. Nicaraguans' standard of living has not improved much. Jobs are scarce, health care prohibitively expensive, and the majority cannot afford to feed and clothe their families. The economy has gradually improved, but it is not enough to alleviate widespread poverty. In Managua for example, new foreign restaurants such as T.G.I. Friday's, have opened. However, few Nicaraguans can afford to dine at these restaurants.

Although textile (clothing) manufacturing is starting to develop, Nicaragua's economy has tradi-tionally been based on agriculture, which accounts for nearly 30 percent of the country's gross domestic product (GDP). Natural resources include fertile soil, a tropical climate, abundant forests, and the oceans. The Sandinistas tried to make Nicaragua a self-sufficient nation by teaching more people how to grow food and giving them land, seeds, and supplies. The Chamorro administration returned much of that land to its pre-revolution owners. Thus landless farmers now try to earn a meager living selling brooms or shining shoes in parking lots outside expensive shopping centers. The current government is encouraging foreign companies to set up operations in Nicaragua, with the hope that they will provide jobs for the people.

Above: **Life goes on for the poor.**

Opposite: **A Nicaraguan woman sells handmade pottery by the roadside.**

A TROUBLED ECONOMY

From 1981 to 1990 the GDP fell an average of 1.5 percent yearly. Per capita income (the average income) fell by an annual average of 4.1 percent during the same period, reaching a low of $300 in 1989. In 1988, inflation was estimated to be between 2,000 and 36,000 percent. These figures reflect the economic problems caused by conflicts, the U.S. trade embargo, changes in trade, floods, drought, and fluctuating commodity prices.

When Chamorro took office in 1990, she introduced a new currency. The córdoba oro started off equal to the U.S. dollar, but by May 1993 the exchange rate was 5 córdobas to the dollar. The exchange rate in 2005 was about 16 córdobas to the dollar.

Just as the country was recovering from the effects of the civil war in the 1980s, Hurricane Mitch devastated the country in 1998, followed by the worldwide collapse in the price of coffee, Nicaragua's most important export. The economy has shown some signs of recovery since the late 1990s, with lower inflation and some growth in GDP, and the country's poverty rate dropped 4.5 percent from 1993 to 2001. The bad news is that 48 percent of the country still lives in poverty.

AGRICULTURE, FISHERIES, AND FORESTRY

Agriculture has been Nicaragua's leading economic activity. Revenue from agriculture makes up nearly 30 percent of the country's GDP, and about 42 percent of the country's workforce does some type of agricultural work. Nicaragua grows the majority of its own food, and most of the farming that is done is subsistence farming. That is, the farmer produces just enough food to feed the family. There is seldom a surplus to sell, so the family is usually destined to poverty. Bad weather or bad luck can quickly lead to hunger.

The córdoba oro or gold córdoba.

One problem with agriculture has been the issue of land ownership. After taking office in 1990, the Chamorro administration reversed the Sandinistas' policy of nationalizing land by returning it to its original owners. But the process of returning land to previous owners is a complicated issue, as it deprives the poor of essential farm land, while previous owners may have received their land through connections with powerful dictators. No one yet knows what the right balance is between private land ownership and popular demands for a right to land based on need.

In Nicaragua land means wealth, as agriculture is an important economic activity.

Coffee is vital to Nicaragua's economy and is the biggest export item. Billions of pounds of coffee are sold to the United States, Europe, and Japan. Unfortunately, in the late 1990s, the price of coffee fell drastically due to a glut in the coffee supply. Coffee workers could no longer support their families because the price they got for their coffee was so low. Nicaragua exported $161 million worth of coffee in 2000 but only $86 million in 2003. Things are starting to look up because Nicaragua has focused efforts on developing a specialty in production of organic coffees. Over 200,000 people are currently employed in the coffee growing industry.

Cattle production has grown steadily since 1998 and is now almost as important as coffee as an export item. Fisheries represented 1.5 percent of the GDP in 2003. Shrimp is farmed in the estuaries of Nicaragua's Pacific coast, while lobster is another export item. In 2003 forestry contributed 1 percent to Nicaragua's GDP. Tropical hardwoods, such as mahogany, are exported as logs and used in local furniture manufacture.

Managua, the capital, is also the industrial and commercial center.

INDUSTRY

Although Nicaragua remains heavily dependent on agriculture, agriculture's share of GDP has been decreasing steadily in recent years, while industry and services have been increasing. Industry now contributes 25.4 percent and the service sector nearly 46 percent to Nicaragua's GDP.

In 2003, 29 percent of exports were manufactured goods, of which three-quarters were made up of processed foods such as beer, rum, milk, and cheese. Leather, wood products, and cardboard cartons were other export items. Petroleum refining and distribution is also a major industry.

Nicaragua has a free trade zone, with 65 different businesses and more than 58,000 workers, that operates under special rules giving exporters tax breaks and other benefits. Most of these businesses make clothes or cigars. Net exports from the free trade zones in 2003 were approximately $150 million. Nicaragua is also preparing to be a part of the Central American Free Trade Agreement (CAFTA).

When the price of gold and silver makes it profitable, Nicaragua also exports gold extracted from mines in the Northern Atlantic Autonomous Region and in the central highlands. Nicaragua exported $35 million in gold in 2003, up from $29 million in 2000.

FREE TRADE VERSUS FAIR TRADE

The Central American Free Trade Agreement is a trade arrangement between the United States and the Central American countries of Costa Rica, El Salvador, Guatemala, Honduras, and Nicaragua. The final terms were still being negotiated in 2005, but the goal of the agreement is the creation of a free trade area, similar to the one already in existence between the United States, Canada, and  Mexico, that has fewer tariffs and trade restrictions between member countries. The U.S. government hopes that free trade, which will make exporting and importing more profitable for the nations involved and will create economic opportunity and help promote democracy in these countries. CAFTA is also seen as a stepping stone toward the Free Trade Area of the Americas (FTAA), which would also encompass South American and Caribbean nations (except Cuba).

The pact is opposed by those who worry that factory workers might be poorly paid in these types of arrangements, and that small farmers could be pushed aside to make way for more industrial-style farming. Opponents also say that free trade encourages companies to relocate to countries where environmental standards are not enforced. However, given that Nicaragua is so poor, CAFTA is seen as offering hope, even with its drawbacks. Supporters of CAFTA say that protection for small farms in Nicaragua are built into the CAFTA. They claim it will also enable more women, most of whom have little education, to find work beyond selling food (*above*) or trinkets by the roadside.

Those who feel free trade is unfair to Nicaraguan workers and bad for the environment have proposed an alternative called fair trade. Fair trade is built on the premise that some customers are willing to pay a higher price for products that are manufactured using methods that do not degrade the environment and that give the workers a good wage and good working conditions. Many specialty coffee products from Nicaragua are sold with a fair trade label.

FOREIGN DEBT RELIEF

Long-term success for Nicaragua requires attracting new businesses, creating jobs, and reducing poverty. Nicaragua must improve the country's infrastructure, such as roads, overcome corruption, resolve property rights issues, and continue to increase its foreign trade. This process got a big boost in January 2004 when Nicaragua met conditions to have over 80 percent of its foreign debt forgiven under the Heavily Indebted Poor Countries (HIPC) initiative. According to the economic and political conditions of the program, the excised debt of at least $100 million must be used to reduce poverty.

Nicaragua's economy looks likely to remain feeble even with debt reduction. The economy is still propped up by both foreign aid and remittances. Nicaragua is the second most remittance-dependent country in Latin America on a per capita basis. Attracting new investors is a challenge under current conditions, which favor corruption and inefficiency.

Children in the city of Matagalpa eat their lunch, which is prepared from supplies donated by the Japanese government to help families of farmers affected by floods or droughts.

DEBT RELIEF

Over the years, Nicaragua borrowed lots of money from foreign countries to finance government activities, such as road building, education, and environmental protection. This debt was highest during the Sandinista administration (1979–90), when it rose to $12 billion. It was lowered to $6 billion (or $2,500 per person) during the Chamorro years, and in 2003 it equaled $1,573 per person. Then in 2004 much of Nicaragua's debt burden was forgiven; it is now approximately $463 per person.

EMPLOYMENT AND WAGES

While the installation of a free market economy allowed entrepreneurs to start new businesses and revitalize old ones, the majority lacked the training, skills, and organization to take full advantage of the unfamiliar capitalist system. Many workers lost their jobs when Chamorro sold under-productive industries formerly owned by the Sandinista government to wealthy private citizens. In February 1992 unemployment was reported at 40 percent, and by August it had gone up to 60 percent.

As the economy began to stabilize, the situation improved, but it is still not good. In the early 2000s, unemployment had settled around 20 percent. By 2004 the number of unemployed combined with those underemployed (well-trained workers who take unskilled, low-wage jobs) was at least 40 percent. Some workers try to make ends meet by becoming street vendors who sell food, clothing, newspapers, or anything else they can get their hands on. Nicaragua has a national minimum wage, but the law is not enforced. Even if you did earn the minimum wage, it doesn't meet the cost of basic goods and services in Managua. In 2004 the minimum wage was $46 a month. The average teacher's salary is only about $70 per month.

REMITTANCES

About 300,000 to 500,000 Nicaraguans have escaped the bad times in Nicaragua by immigrating to the United States. They send money to their relatives who did not immigrate. This money is called a remittance. In 2001 Nicaraguans overseas sent home over $600 million, about 25 percent of the GDP. In 2003 this amounted to 20 percent of the GDP. This money provides better housing, education, and lifestyle for those left behind. But some experts worry that this money makes the people left behind lazy.

Nicaragua owes billions of dollars to countries that have provided it with loans. The government is hoping for outright donations in the future.

51

ENVIRONMENT

NICARAGUA'S POLITICAL and economic problems, combined with frequent natural disasters, have made it difficult for the country to effectively protect the environment. Forests are cut and industry pollutes water because rules are not enforced, and residents are forced by poverty to overuse the land.

In Nicaragua, unsightly trash is seen throughout the cities and towns, an obvious sign that most of the general public does not yet fully understand the importance of keeping the country's ecosystems undamaged for the benefit of future generations. Deforestation, soil erosion, and water pollution are the most urgent problems.

Above: **An orchid growing in the tropical forests of Nicaragua**

Opposite: **A large number of waterbirds, such as herons, egrets, and cormorants can be found on Lake Nicaragua.**

PROTECTING NICARAGUA'S DIVERSITY

Despite this neglect, Nicaragua is still rich in beauty and biological diversity with much of the land still undeveloped. A low population density means there is a relatively low level of pollution in most of the country. The key now will be for Nicaragua to be able to use its natural resources in a way that is good for the environment and the people living there. The government and international organizations that help the country, such as the United Nations and the World Bank, are working to help conserve habitat, marine resources, and aquatic life.

Although money and technology may be lacking, the Nicaraguan government is aware of the issues it faces. The Ministry of Environment and Natural Resources is in charge of regulating and protecting the country's environment. Nicaragua has joined other countries in addressing the global challenge of environmental protection.

In Nicaragua many farmers practice slash-and-burn agriculture, which involves burning a patch of the forest to obtain a piece of land for growing crops. After a few years, the farmland becomes infertile and the farmers move on to clear another section of the forest. However, instead of allowing the old farmland to eventually return to forest, the farmers sell the infertile land to ranchers, whose livestock deplete the land further by overgrazing.

CONSERVATION IN NICARAGUA

During the Somoza years, little thought was given to protecting the environment. Instead, the dictatorship wanted to take advantage of the country's resources to gain wealth. As a result, some of Nicaragua's lakes and rivers were polluted with pesticides, raw sewage, and industrial waste, and many of the forests were cut down. Under the Sandinistas, the government started extensive programs to restore and protect the environment. Many of these programs, while they sounded good, turned out to be inefficient and not very well thought-out. Governments since then have tried to find the right balance, but progress is slow.

Fortunately, many nongovernmental organizations (NGOs) have stepped in to support Nicaragua's efforts to conserve its natural resources. NGOs, such as the World Wildlife Fund and the Nature Conservancy, provide experts to work on scientific studies and money to pay for park rangers and equipment. NGOs also help fund educational projects that teach Nicaraguans the importance of protecting the environment.

SOME BRIGHT SPOTS

Nicaragua has 76 designated protected areas in the country that cover 18 percent of the land. Large tracts of land that include mountains, rain forests, volcanoes, beaches, and reefs remain isolated from human intrusion and are home to unique plants and animals. Scientists and conservationists dream of keeping it that way.

Nicaragua, as the largest country in Central America, holds a vital place in what biologists call the Mesoamerican Biological Corridor. A biological corridor is an area of land that connects habitats over a long distance. Mesoamerica is an area of land that stretches from southern Mexico to Panama. It covers just 0.5 percent of the earth's land area, but is home to nearly 10 percent of the world's known species. Monkeys, harpy eagles, and several species of sea turtles still live here. American manatees, Central American tapirs, Central American woolly opossums, giant anteaters, and Honduran fruit-eating bats are some of the other endangered animals living in this area.

In this decade, six natural reserves—two in the mountains and four in the Pacific region—received special funding from the international community to improve their management. The goal was to find a way to start managing these reserves cooperatively, because Nicaragua's government does not have the funds or expertise to manage them on its own.

A partnership between local and national governments, international groups, and others are putting Nicaraguan university students to work in some of these preserves. Not only do the students earn money to complete their education, they also learn how to play an important role in the preservation of their country's natural resources. The new management system also encourages local residents to help decide how to conserve the habitat, since, unlike the park system in many countries, most of these protected areas are on privately owned, not public, lands.

This type of cooperation is coming just in time. Over one-third of the country is covered by forests, but logging is shrinking this by 400 square miles (1,036 square km) a year. Most logging in Nicaragua is either partly or totally illegal. Logging can be done in a way that benefits both the forest and the people, but instead, Nicaragua's forests are gradually being destroyed. The loss of revenue to Nicaragua's GDP from illegal logging is estimated to be about $4 million to $8 million a year.

A group of Nicaraguan schoolgirls in the country's highlands take in the view of a caldera lake, which was formed by rainwater filling in a crater.

ECOTOURISM

Ecotourists kayak on Lake Nicaragua.

Unlike its neighbor Costa Rica, Nicaragua has not enjoyed much tourism. Nicaragua's government sees tourism as a path out of poverty and is encouraging the growth of ecofriendly tourism. Ecotourism brings in jobs and money, and it serves to protect wildlife habitats. Visitors can hike through wildlife-filled rain forests, climb sulfur-spitting volcanoes, spend a few nights at a lodge located in the forest, and roam miles of undeveloped shoreline knowing that the money they spend on their visit is helping to preserve what they are enjoying.

A number of new tourism projects are designed to help local people directly. Not only do tourists get to enjoy the pristine environment and beauty of Nicaragua's natural areas, but their money provides work and a stable income for local residents, as well as enabling local children to attend school.

IMPORTANT WATERWAYS UNDER THREAT

Lake Managua (also known as Lake Xolotlán) is Nicaragua's second-largest lake. At 36 miles (58 km) long and 16 miles (25 km) wide, with cone-shaped volcanoes rising on the edges, Lake Managua is an impressive sight. Sadly, it is severely polluted with industrial, residential, and agricultural waste. Few people dare to swim or fish in the lake, and resources to clean it are inadequate.

The larger Lake Nicaragua, or Lake Cocibolca, with an area of 3,149 square miles (8,157 square km), is the second largest lake in Latin America after Lake Titicaca on the border of Peru and Bolivia. Lake Nicaragua is connected to the Caribbean Sea by the Río San Juan along Nicaragua's

LAKE NICARAGUA-RÍO SAN JUAN WATERSHED

The lands of the Lake Nicaragua-Río San Juan watershed include numerous types of ecosystems (a watershed is the region of land where the water drains into a specified body of water). The areas to the east, north, and west of Lake Nicaragua are covered with dry tropical forest. This important lower-elevation habitat has a large variety of trees, and many of them shed their leaves during the dry season. At one time, dry tropical forest covered much of Central America's Pacific coast from Mexico to Panama, but most of it has been cut down for agricultural use.

South and southwest of Lake Nicaragua, the land receives more rain. Here, in the tropical rain forest, palms and ferns grow alongside an amazing variety of tree species, some growing to great heights. Other species grow below the tallest trees in a series of green layers. Mahogany and cedar are common, but dozens of other lesser-known species also occur here.

A part of the San Juan Watershed extends across the border into Costa Rica. Here the watershed includes the upper elevations of a volcanic mountain range, and at the top of these mountains is a cloud forest. Cloud forests are wet and are covered in fog and clouds most of the time. These highlands have an abundance of moss, ferns, and plants called epiphytes that grow on trees. Orchids are the most well-known type of epiphytes.

Along the banks of the Río San Juan grows a special type of forest called gallery forest. Here ficus, balsa wood, and other species of trees thrive in the humid conditions, and they can withstand periodic flooding. In the shallow, fresh water along the lakes, rivers, and estuaries of the watershed, fragile wetlands harbor many species of aquatic birds and provide nesting places for fish, reptiles, and amphibians. Finally, where the watershed meets the sea, mangrove swamps flourish in flooded coastal areas; these highly specialized ecosystems are home to a high number of saltwater-loving animal species, such as the mangrove crab. Usually the only trees in these swamps are the low-growing, evergreen mangroves, which are well-adapted to their salty and swampy habitat.

border with Costa Rica. The area surrounding the lake and river is known as the Lake Nicaragua-Río San Juan watershed. Located in the center of Central America's biological corridor, this is where the ecosystems of North and South America come together, giving the Río San Juan basin a rich biological diversity. So far, the watershed has remained relatively unpolluted, but the area is coming under increasing pressure from human activity; residue from pesticides and other agrochemical substances affect the purity of this fresh water supply. Natural calamities, such as hurricanes and earthquakes also threaten the water quality.

In 2005 the governments of Costa Rica and Nicaragua worked together on several projects designed to clean up pollution, treat wastewater, and promote ecotourism and fishing.

PROTECTED AREAS

Nicaragua is striving to protect as much of its natural heritage as it can. Nicaragua currently has over 70 protected areas; the most important either protect remaining large areas of undeveloped land or target specific endangered species or habitats.

Indio-Maíz Biological Reserve (1,019 square miles or 2,639 square km) is one of the few remaining virgin tropical forests in Central America. Not only is this preserve home to ocelots and jaguars, but it also boasts more than 400 species of birds and over 200 species of reptiles.

Bosawás Biosphere Reserve, along Nicaragua's northern border with Honduras, is one of Nicaragua's largest (282 square miles or 730.4 square km) and least visited natural areas. This isolation makes the reserve's cloud forest a perfect hideaway for 12 kinds of poisonous snakes.

Cayos Miskitos Biological Reserve, a group of islands near the northern Caribbean coast, offers a refuge to manatees and sea turtles that swim through extensive coral reefs. Rare and endangered species here include the green turtle, the hawksbill turtle, and a species of freshwater dolphin. The rare shark *Rhizoprionodon porosus*, or Caribbean sharpnose shark, is found here, too. The islands are so remote that it takes five hours by boat to get to the islands from the nearest town.

Around 30 years ago, Nicaragua's neighbor, Costa Rica, devoted much time and effort to protect its mountains and cloud forest habitats. Now it is considered one of the world's top nature destinations. But this popularity has its disadvantages: crowds and high prices. Nicaragua, on the other hand, fought civil wars and suffered poverty during the same period. These problems kept land developers and tourists away, so the current condition of Nicaragua's Miraflor Nature Reserve is said to be just like Costa Rica's cloud forests 30 years ago. The 128-square-mile (150-

square-km) Miraflor Nature Reserve harbors the legendary bird of Central America, the quetzal, plus 300 species of orchids, beautiful waterfalls, and monkeys.

Juan Venado Island Natural Reserve is an important barrier island on the Pacific coast. Barrier islands are narrow sandy pieces of land that run parallel to the mainland, built up by the action of waves and currents. These islands protect the coast from erosion by surf and tidal surges. In this case, the 20-mile (32.3-km)-long island also serves as an important nesting area for thousands of parrots and herons.

Mombacho Volcano Reserve is a dormant cone-shaped volcano. The volcano is located on a 30-square-mile (77.7-square-km) island that is covered with forest and coffee plantations, and is home to monkeys, butterflies, and a species of salamander (*Bolitoglossa mombachoensis*) found nowhere else. Because it is located on the shore of Lake Nicaragua near the popular tourist town of Granada, Mombacho is a popular hiking spot.

The Masaya Volcano Park is very close to Managua and is one of Nicaragua's most visited natural areas. The park offers easy road access to the top of a low volcano, which is surrounded by a 20-square-mile (52-square-km) dry tropical forest.

Although it covers only 3 square miles (7.77 square km) along Nicaragua's southern Pacific coast, La Flor Wildlife Refuge is one of the most important turtle nesting grounds in the country. Between July and January, thousands of sea turtles lay eggs in holes that they dig in the sand. Farther inland, the crescent of white sand gradually gives way to dry tropical forest.

A male resplendent quetzal bears food for its nestlings. The tail of the male bird can reach up to 2 feet (60 cm) in length. The quetzal was revered by the Mayas, who used its feathers in ceremonial and royal costumes.

NICARAGUANS

NICARAGUANS, or Nicas, as they like to call themselves, are typically friendly and generous people. Despite the poverty-stricken condition of their country, Nicaraguans keep their spirits up and face the nation's economic and political problems with a willingness to make the best of a bad situation. Even in the worst situations, anyone who has food will share with someone who is hungry, and Nicaraguans never hesitate to open their homes to visitors. Visiting American anthropologists and writers report that they received the same hospitality that the locals do. And Nicaraguans love to talk. They share stories, talk about their families, and gossip about what goes on around the neighborhood. They generally display a strong pride in their homeland, and their nationality is very important to them.

Nicaraguans have different ethnic origins. The majority of the people are mestizos, peoples of mixed Spanish and indigenous ancestry, but several other ethnic groups make up the rest of the population: indigenous peoples, Creoles, black Caribs, and Spaniards. Most of the indigenous groups, Creoles, and blacks live in the eastern part of Nicaragua, while the western part is inhabited mainly by mestizos. Nicaragua's geography makes it hard to get from one coast to the other, so people identify more with the region they live in than with the nation as a whole. The distance between the two coasts has resulted in regional loyalties and characteristics.

Above: **Despite Nicaragua's political and economic problems, adults and children alike have resigned themselves to making the best of a bad situation.**

Opposite: **Two young girls in traditional costumes in the southwestern city of Rivas.**

POPULATION FACTS: A COMPARISON

	Nicaragua	United States
Population	5,359,759	293,027,571
Urban population	57 percent	80 percent
Age distribution: 0–14	38.1 percent	20.8 percent
15–59	58.9 percent	66.9 percent
60 & over	3 percent	12.4 percent
Population growth	1.97 percent	0.92 percent
Population density (people per square km)	44	32
Life expectancy: men	68	75
women	72	80
Infant mortality (per 1,000 live births)	30.15	6.63

Women are an important part of the workforce.

ETHNIC GROUPS

Six minority groups live mainly along the Atlantic coast: Miskitos, Ramas, and Sumos (also known as Sumus) are aboriginal people whose ancestors were natives of the land before Spanish colonization; Creoles are of mixed European and African descent; and Garífunas and black Caribs have a mix of indigenous and African ancestry. Although the remoteness of the Atlantic coast makes it hard to conduct an accurate census of the area, estimates from 2003 place Nicaragua's minority, or non-mestizo, population at about 14 percent, and most of these minorities live on the Atlantic coast.

Of the estimated 750,366 minority population in Nicaragua, nearly 70 percent are Miskitos. In the 17th and 18th centuries, the Miskito nation expanded by conquering other aboriginal people. By 1850 they occupied the entire Mosquito Coast, which extends from Panama in the south to Honduras in the north. In the past, Miskitos practiced small-scale farming and fishing, as well as performing some seasonal salaried labor for foreign-owned companies. Today Miskitos are involved in local government and work in most sectors of the economy.

Around 10,000 Sumos live in small isolated communities along the coast and in a few larger villages in the Bambana River basin. Many Sumo communities were taken over by the Miskitos in the 17th and 18th centuries. An even smaller group is the Rama, only about 1,000 of whom still live in Nicaragua. They live on Rama Cay, a small island in the Bay of Bluefields, and in Monkey Point, a village south of Bluefields. In the 18th century, they moved frequently to avoid being captured by Miskitos and sold to the British as slaves.

A modern whitewashed church in Bluefields, where most Creoles and Garífunas live.

Around 25 percent of the non-mestizo population in Nicaragua have some African ancestry, and most of them live on the Atlantic Coast. Black Caribs first came to the area as slaves from British colonies in the West Indies. They remained there after slavery was abolished in 1824 and today live mainly in the Laguna de Perlas area.

Creoles are people of African and Spanish, or other European, descent. The British brought Africans to the coast in the 17th century to work as slaves on their plantations. When the British lost control of the region, many Africans stayed. Around the same time, Jamaican merchants began arriving on the coast. In the 19th century U.S. lumber and banana companies attracted blacks from the southern United States and the Antilles Islands in the West Indies. Today most Creoles live in Bluefields and the surrounding area. Many are skilled or semiskilled workers, and some are office employees, technicians, or professionals.

Fishing is a thriving industry along the eastern coast, which overlooks the Caribbean Sea.

Garífunas resemble blacks in physical appearance, but their culture derives from several Latin American indigenous groups. Their ancestors lived on the islands of St. Vincent and Dominica until the Carib War (1795–97). After the war, the British sent the survivors to an island in the Bay of Honduras. Over half the people died during the trip; only about 2,000 arrived safely. Later, the Garífunas migrated to Nicaragua for better jobs in the mahogany industry and on banana plantations. Most of the 3,000 Garífunas in Nicaragua today live at Laguna de Perlas and Bluefields.

Even on the Atlantic side of Nicaragua, mestizos make up the majority of the population. They are concentrated in the northern department of Zelaya. They began moving east during the second half of the 19th century and founded the small town of Rama, which became an important center of commerce.

CULTURAL DIFFERENCES

Nicaragua's two coasts are like two separate countries. People on one side know little about life on the other. The natural resources of the two areas are quite different, resulting in dissimilar lifestyles. Farmers on the Pacific side of the country know a lot about growing coffee and corn, while those in the east grow mainly coconuts and bananas. The main industries along the Caribbean coast are fishing and catching lobsters. On the Pacific coast there are many more schools, colleges, and businesses. In the east, many indigenous people still follow the traditions and customs of their ancestors.

The people who live on the Caribbean are called *costeños* (koh-STÉN-nohs; which means coastal people) by the residents of the Pacific side of

A black child of the
Atlantic coast.

Nicaragua, but sharing a name does not mean these diverse groups of people share a culture. Each group has its own language, culture, and traditions, all of which are a mystery to most of the residents of western Nicaragua. The *costeños* do not know much about the people from the Pacific side of the country either. They call them Spaniards, and worry that more and more will move to the east and bring with them their language, music, and food, diluting the *costeños'* cultural traditions.

Ethnic identity became an important issue only recently. Past governments mostly ignored the Caribbean coast, but when the Sandinistas came to power, they guaranteed civil rights for the non-mestizos and made ethnic identity a political issue. They promoted respect for traditional indigenous religions, languages, and celebrations but sometimes offended the indigenous people by trying to integrate them with the rest of Nicaragua. What the indigenous people really wanted was independence and control of the abundant natural resources in the region. Peace between the government and the indigenous people came when the Sandinistas helped organize an autonomous local government to regulate life on the Caribbean coast.

"Viva Daniel"—probably a reference to Daniel Ortega, the former Sandinista president and current leader of the FSLN—is scrawled on the wall of this middle-class urban home.

SOCIAL STRUCTURE

Throughout the 20th century, distinct social classes have existed in Nicaraguan culture. During the Somoza dictatorship, a very small upper class owned almost 80 percent of the land, while the rest of the people were poor, landless, and struggling to feed their families. In the 1970s over half the people earned only $250 each year. People were very rich or very poor; there was virtually no middle class.

After the revolution, the Sandinistas tried to shrink the gap between the rich and the poor by redistributing land confiscated from large landowners to peasants. However, the Contras specifically targeted and attacked farms and other food production facilities, destroying the Sandinistas' efforts. In the last 15 years, the country has tried to make capitalism work, and many wealthy upper-class people have gotten their land back.

Over the last decade or so, a fairly large middle class has emerged, consisting of families who have the basic necessities and maybe a few luxuries, such as a refrigerator or relatively new clothes. Usually, these families need two incomes to maintain their lifestyle. Most Nicaraguans would probably be considered working class, which means they have to work hard just to make ends meet. They are not poor, but they earn only enough money to buy food and other essentials. Many other people in the country still live in poverty.

How much power and opportunity people have usually depends on their job. Farmers

Nicaraguans lining up for visas to travel to the United States.

usually do not have much political power, and they do not have many opportunities to advance to a higher social standing. The Sandinistas tried unsuccessfully to change this fact of Nicaraguan life, but the main factor that determines what kind of jobs people will have is the family they are born into. Many families have been poor for generations, and they often feel that there is no way to change their lives.

Unfortunately, this is usually true. It is hard for children of poor farmers to grow up to be wealthy business owners, for example. Often they do not finish school in order to help with the farm work. Children born to wealthy parents, on the other hand, have a much better chance of attending private schools or finishing their education in foreign countries. In Nicaragua, wealth equals power, and power brings opportunity.

LEAVING THEIR HOMELAND

Although Nicaraguans possess a strong love of their homeland, economic problems and natural calamities have induced many to seek refuge in other countries. The effects of Hurricane Mitch and the fall of coffee prices in the late 1990s sent a large influx of Nicaraguans across the border into Costa Rica in search of work. However, between 1979 and 1990, somewhere between 5 percent and 15 percent of the population left Nicaragua because of conflicts between the government and opposition forces. (Estimates vary greatly because some include only refugees and exiles, while others also count the Contras and their families who left when the Sandinistas took over.) Contra attacks along the Caribbean coast caused about 40,000 Miskitos and Sumos to flee to Costa Rica and Honduras. Of those who left, over 30 percent were students or other draft-age men. Many men left Nicaragua during the Sandinista control to avoid mandatory military service. Some went to other Central American countries, some to Europe, some to various parts of the United States, but by far, the largest concentration of migrant Nicaraguans is in Miami, Florida.

LIFE IN MIAMI The Nicaraguan community in Miami is made up of different cultures, just like in Nicaragua. There are the Creole and Miskito peoples of the southern Atlantic coast, and the mestizos of the Pacific coast. Echoing the situation in Nicaragua, these communities do not have much contact since their cultural heritages are so different. The timing and reasons behind their arrival in Miami are different, too. Many of the Creole population came to study in the United States as early as the 1950s. The Miskitos, on the other hand, fled Nicaragua during the Contra war, when they were mistreated by both sides. Large numbers of mestizos lived in Miami even before the revolution of 1979.

In Miami, Florida Nicaraguans continue to celebrate many of their traditional festivals that honor Catholic saints, but with a few changes. Instead of being held on the actual saint's day, they celebrate on the closest Sunday to the true holiday, and all festivities occur in a single day, instead of over a week or more.

FAMOUS NICARAGUANS

RUBÉN DARÍO was born Félix Rubén García Sarmiento in the village of Metapa on January 18, 1867. He became one of the most famous Central American poets and led the modernist movement in poetry, which rejuvenated traditional Spanish romantic poems by adding a dimension of expressive rhythm. In 1888 he published *Blue*, a revolutionary and prophetic work that marked the official birth of modernism. Darío died on February 6, 1916, in Nicaragua.

PEDRO JOAQUÍN CHAMORRO CARDENAL was born in Granada on September 23, 1924. He came from a family that included four former presidents; his great-granduncle of the same name was Nicaragua's first president. Chamorro studied at the Central American University in Managua and later went to the National Autonomous University in Mexico to study law. His father, Pedro Joaquín Chamorro Zelaya, owned a newspaper called *La Prensa*. When his father died in 1952, Chamorro became the paper's director. As publisher and editor of *La Prensa* throughout the 1960s, he used the paper to tell the people about the injustices of the Somoza regime. He married Violeta Barrios Torres (president of Nicaragua, 1990–1998) on December 8, 1950. Chamorro was assassinated on January 10, 1978, at age 53.

JOSÉ CARLOS FONSECA AMADOR was born in Matagalpa on June 23, 1936, to working-class parents Fausto F. Amador and Justina Fonseca. As a boy, he helped his mother by peddling the candy she made and selling newspapers on the street. After grade school, he worked for two months before entering secondary school. In 1955 he graduated with a gold medal awarded to the best student each year. He then went to law school at the National University. In the early 1960s, he and two others founded the FSLN. He was imprisoned many times for his involvement with various antigovernment youth movements. He was killed in combat on November 8, 1976.

BIANCA JAGGER (*above*) was born Bianca Pérez Morena De Macias in Managua. She won a scholarship to study at the Paris Institute of Political Studies. While in Paris, she met British rock star Mick Jagger. They married in 1971, but were divorced in 1979. Today, Jagger uses her fame to boost awareness of Nicaragua's environmental issues as well as the plight of the indigenous people in Central America. She has also directed a documentary film about her homeland. She continues to work for human rights throughout the world. In 2004 Jagger received the World Achievement Award for her commitment to human rights, social and economic justice, and environmental causes.

LIFESTYLE

LIVING IN NICARAGUAN CITIES means always being around lots of other people, but out in the mountains and countryside, families can live miles from the next house. Some people are very poor, while others are very wealthy. People support the government, or they fight to change it. For all these reasons, many different lifestyles exist in Nicaragua. But no matter where they live, how much money they have, or which political party they support, all Nicaraguans place tremendous importance on the family.

Certain aspects of Nicaraguan life are changing as the country develops. As a whole, the nation is behind the times compared to the United States, Great Britain, and other technologically and culturally developed countries. Part of the problem in recent times is that no political party has stayed in power long enough to establish an effective system of government. At the same time, corruption has seen little money devoted to improving the people's lives. The current government is working to reduce corruption and create a capitalist, free-market system in an attempt to stabilize the economy. Some people are better off now than they were five years ago, but many others remain stuck in poverty.

Culturally, some changes for the better are starting to improve life for young people. For example, many now continue their education beyond primary school. They think about race, class, and gender relations and ways to make their country a better place to live. They appear to realize that they can make a difference in their country's future.

Above: **Like this woman, most Nicaraguans dress in light, cool cotton.**

Opposite: **A Nicaraguan woman on Ometepe Island does her laundry in the waters of Lake Nicaragua.**

Lack of proper sanitation in some parts, especially in shantytowns, contribute to the spread of disease.

LIVING CONDITIONS

Nearly 60 percent of Nicaraguans live in cities, and every day many more are exchanging rural living for the urban life. Many people move to the cities, especially Managua, hoping to find better jobs. There are eight large cities. The three largest are Managua (population 1,113,100), León (population 147,800), and Chinandega (population 125,500). Other cities include Granada, Masaya, Matagalpa, Estelí, and Jinotepe.

Most cities have well-planned residential areas with gardens, parks, a market, and shopping centers, but nearly all of them also have barrios, or poorer neighborhoods where houses are crowded with people, small, and close together. One can usually tell how much money a family has by looking at the floor of their home. Poor people have dirt floors, while working- and middle-class people have cemented or tiled ones. Nearly half the people who are capable of working cannot find jobs or are underemployed, that is they work at jobs that do not completely utilize their skills.

None of the governments since 1990 have made much progress in providing better living conditions for the poor. During Alemán's administration, the economy improved, but in recent years, bad weather and falling prices for the country's most important export products have led to severe hardship, hunger, and malnutrition for many citizens. In 2002, 43.5 percent of homes had a dirt floor, and only 22.6 percent had indoor plumbing. On the other hand, key improvements show that Nicaraguans are still striving for a better future. The country's poverty rate dropped 4.5 percent from 1993 to 2001, life expectancy rose, and the infant mortality rate fell from 52 per 1,000 births in 1990 to 32 per 1,000 in 2002.

GETTING AROUND AND STAYING IN TOUCH

Until recently, only the main streets in big cities were paved. Cars were scarce, and most people got from place to place by walking or taking a bus. Today Nicaragua has more cars and more paved streets, but horse-drawn cabs and dirt roads are still common. Public transportation is fairly cheap, but it is slow and overcrowded. Car ownership is much more common now than in the past. The majority of car owners live in the largest cities, where most roads are paved. Drivers face hazards, though, such as potholes in the roads, plus a mix of slow-moving traffic that includes pedestrians, bicycles, and horse carts.

Vendors crowd around a bus to sell beer and candies to passengers.

Finding your way around can be tricky. Neighborhoods have names but most streets do not, so asking for directions does not help much. Also, Nicaraguans say, "Go toward the lake" or "Go up" instead of "Head south" or "Go left." While other Nicaraguans usually understand because they know where "the lake" is, these directions often seem vague and confusing to foreigners.

Nicaraguans usually live close to their relatives. It is not unusual for several families living in the same neighborhood to be related. Living close together means they do not have to go far to borrow a cup of sugar or find someone to help carry a heavy load. People help each other out all the time by lending food, giving advice, and doing favors. For families living farther apart, the occasional phone call keeps them in touch.

Washing clothes is often an outdoor affair.

URBAN PROBLEMS

As Nicaraguan cities continue to grow, urban problems caused by a lack of employment and necessities become harder to control. Poverty and crime go together, especially in cities, and Nicaragua has plenty of both. Alcoholism and drug violence account for an increasing percentage of the crime rate in the country.

Crime and random violence are also on the rise. Violent crime in Managua and other cities is also increasing, and street crimes, such as pickpocketing, are common. Worried about muggings, residents are careful about where they go at night. Occasional armed robberies and even murders occur on crowded buses, at bus stops, and in open markets, particularly the large Mercado Oriental. Gang activity is starting to get a foothold in Managua, although gang violence is much lower than in neighboring countries, accounting for less than 1 percent of all violent crimes.

Car theft is another concern. Even if drivers lock their doors, thieves will sometimes take valuable parts, such as mirrors, spare tires, and hubcaps, from unattended vehicles. All public parking lots, such as at supermarkets or restaurants, are attended by guards who keep an eye on cars while their owners are shopping. At some smaller businesses, children earn a little money by charging a small fee to watch a car until the owner returns.

Although the crime rate is increasing, Nicaragua has a crime rate lower than the other Central American countries.

FAMILIES

The average family has four or five children, and poor rural families often have seven or eight. Households usually include uncles, aunts, cousins, or grandparents. Often, with three or four generations living in the same house, children are indulged as well as disciplined. Parents typically believe that spanking or beating their children with a belt is an acceptable form of punishment, but mothers and grandmothers are also generous with praise, hugs, and other gestures of affection.

Nicaraguans place a great deal of importance on maintaining close family relationships. Many couples, especially in rural areas, live together and raise families without getting a marriage license (which costs money and requires travel to a city). This arrangement is called a common-law marriage. But most people in the cities, women especially, see the benefits of a legal marriage, which allows them equal rights to their children and the family's possessions.

Nicaraguans often marry young, some as early as 13. Almost 40 percent of girls ages 15 to 19 are married, and most become mothers at a young age. Teenagers account for nearly 25 percent of all births in Nicaragua, the highest percentage in Central America. Unwed motherhood is also very common. Some young pregnant girls are disowned by their families. The fortunate ones have their families' support, even though the Catholic Church disapproves of unwed pregnancy. In these cases, when the baby is born, it is welcomed into the family and everyone helps to take care of it. Some girls have babies before they are fully ready to start a family. These babies are often raised by their grandmothers, while their mothers finish their education.

Nicaraguans look to their young people to build a better future.

75

DIFFERENT STROKES Boys and girls are treated differently from a young age. Boys are teased and taunted to teach them to be tough, while girls are doted on and treated more gently. When little boys pick up vulgar language, adults are generally amused by it and only punish them if they direct obscenities at adults. Girls, on the other hand, are punished swiftly if they swear. Boys as young as 2 are given small jobs or errands to do, such as going to a neighbor's house to buy ice, but girls are not encouraged to be independent. Teenaged girls must obey strict rules about going out with friends, while boys are allowed to roam the neighborhood even after dusk.

DOUBLE INCOMES Most Nicaraguan families need at least two incomes just to buy enough food. Because it is hard to find a high-paying job, many adults take on two or three odd jobs to supplement the household income. Mothers may work part-time in an office, take in neighbors' laundry, and make candy or tortillas to sell on the street. Sometimes, the father or oldest son leaves home to work in the United States.

Children as young as 5 or 6 often help out on the family farm or work as street vendors. In poor families, the children must contribute in one way or another just so everyone has enough food. Wealthy families, on the other hand, often have several maids to cook, clean, and take care of the children.

A woman with a child in her arms sells bananas to supplement the family income.

MACHISMO

Machismo defines the power structure between women and men. To Nicaraguans, being masculine means being aggressive, while women's roles are associated with being passive. Men love and honor their mothers very much, but do not treat their wives or girlfriends the same way. They can be disrespectful and even abusive toward women. Because household chores and child care are considered women's work, most men refuse to do them.

Other behaviors, such as excessive drinking and getting into fights, are blamed on machismo. Many men think cheating on their wives is permissible because it is in the masculine nature, but this irresponsible conduct causes all kinds of problems. Women in several different households may have children fathered by the same man, and often the father does not support any of them.

Mothers today are raising their sons to help out around the house and treat women with kindness and respect, but often boys are confused, because they still see their fathers acting according to machismo. Since the revolution, however, the idea of what makes a "good" man has slowly begun to change. Now, people are defining a good man as one who is responsible toward his family, works hard, and studies to improve himself and his country.

WOMEN AND MEN

Although Nicaragua has had a woman president, the country has a long history of male supremacy. Women only received the right to vote in 1955, and today, they are still fighting for equality in a country where being female usually means being a second-class citizen. On the other hand, girls and women in Nicaragua have gradually been gaining more independence compared to their counterparts in some other Latin American countries, thanks in part to the continuing Sandinista influence.

Until the revolution, women had fewer rights and opportunities than men, but that did not keep them from joining the fight to overthrow Somoza. Three out of 10 Sandinista soldiers were female. The Sandinista government recognized the important role women played in the revolution and vowed to bring about equality between the genders. One of the first actions of the ruling junta was the passage of an equal-rights law.

Unfortunately, laws cannot change certain facts of Nicaraguan life that make women's lives difficult. Spanish culture has a long tradition of machismo, an attitude of superiority over women that is shared by most men in Nicaragua.

The authorities know that some men beat their wives, but unless a woman reports her husband's violence, the authorities cannot do anything to help. The cultural trait of machismo is so ingrained that some women believe they are inferior to men and see the violence against them as inevitable rather than a wrong.

Most Nicaraguans do not attach the same importance to their jobs as many North Americans or Asians do, but they are not lazy. They just feel that family is the most important part of life, and work is what they have to do to support their family.

FICTIVE KIN AND GODPARENTS

Children in Nicaragua will probably know someone they call "aunt" or "uncle" who is not really related to them but is a close friend of their parents. This kind of relationship, called fictive kinship, is common in Nicaragua. The tradition of *compadrazgo* (kahm-pah-DRAHZ-goh), or coparenting, is another way that Nicaraguans use to expand their families and make sure their children are well taken care of. When a child is born, the parents choose a godmother and a godfather, who become part of the family network. They are expected to assist with the child's moral and religious upbringing, as well as his or her material needs. If the real parents should die, the godparents will take responsibility for the child. Godparents are a source of emotional as well as financial and material support. The two families often exchange favors, advice, food, and clothing, and provide child care support.

People might ask neighbors, friends, relatives, or coworkers to be their children's godparents, and a lot of thought goes into that decision. Ideally they want to choose someone with whom their child will develop a lasting bond, but other considerations are also involved. Parents think about all these things when selecting godparents for each child in the family. They choose:

- neighbors because they can be easily called on for favors;
- relatives or friends with a lot of money, because they can give their godchildren a financial advantage;
- doctors, because if the child or anyone else in the family gets sick, the doctor would be able to help;
- relatives in the United States, because they might send U.S. dollars or items that cannot be bought in Nicaragua; and
- members of the father's family, so that if the father is irresponsible, the child will still get support from the godparent.

HEALTH

Health conditions in Nicaragua are poor compared to more industrialized nations, but they are about the same as in other Central American countries. Mosquito-borne diseases such as malaria and dengue fever are common. One of every four children has some degree of chronic malnutrition and 9 percent suffer from severe malnutrition. People die at a younger age than the average for the rest of the region.

However, Nicaragua does have a lower number of HIV and AIDS cases than the rest of Central America, and the immunization rate against various diseases for children is high (close to 90 percent). There is a trend toward smaller families, which are usually healthier. The population growth rate dropped from 3.1 percent in 1993 to around 2 percent in 2004.

UNICEF estimated that in 2002 around 93 percent of the urban population received clean drinking water as compared to 65 percent of the rural population. Clean drinking water is vital because without it, people end up drinking from the same streams they bathe in and use as a toilet. In the parts of Nicaragua that do not have clean drinking water, some children die of dehydration brought about by diarrhea, which they get from drinking polluted water.

Access to doctors and hospitals in Nicaragua reflects the basic structure of society. Wealthy and middle-class Nicaraguans can afford good, expensive, and private health care. The poor, however, depend on cheaper public hospitals, which have old equipment and poorly trained doctors. Rural areas often have no health care at all, and poor residents have to travel to the nearest city to see a doctor. Managua contains one-fifth of the country's population, but around half of the available health personnel. Most people in the country do not have a car, so getting to the city to visit a clinic or a specialist when they are sick is an expensive ordeal.

Many Nicaraguans in rural areas draw their drinking water from the same streams they bathe and wash in, and this exposes them to the risk of disease.

EDUCATION

Before the revolution, few children went to school and over half of the population could not read or write. Many rural areas had no school. The Somoza regime kept the people ignorant, so that the people would be powerless to effect change. When the Sandinistas took over, they made education a top priority. They built hundreds of schools and launched a teaching campaign that brought literacy rates up to almost 90 percent. School was free and compulsory for children from 6 to 13 years old, and two five-hour sessions were held each day to accommodate them all. Desks were in short supply, and some students carried theirs to and from school so they would not get stolen overnight. Students were expected to help clean up around the school. Younger ones picked up litter and washed lunch tables, while older children shoveled mud to release stagnant pools of water, the breeding ground of disease-carrying mosquitoes.

Unfortunately, the Contras worked just as hard to destroy these efforts. By the end of the Contra war, 411 teachers had been killed. The guerrillas also kidnapped 66 teachers and 59 students, destroyed 46 schools, damaged another 21, and forced the temporary closure of over 550.

THE LITERACY CRUSADE

Perhaps the biggest achievement of the Sandinistas was their success in educating Nicaraguans. As soon as Somoza was defeated, the Sandinistas set up adult education programs and vocational and technical training centers. But their pet project was the Literacy Crusade.

Organizers of the Literacy Crusade called upon everyone over 12 years old who had completed elementary education to help teach reading and writing to thousands of illiterate Nicaraguans. Schools were closed to prepare the young volunteers, called *brigadistas* (bree-gah-DEEZ-tahs), for the monumental task. In April 1980, after extensive physical, mental, and emotional training, around 80,000 *brigadistas* were ready.

About 55,000 volunteers went off to the mountains and other rural places to teach the *campesinos* (kahm-peh-SEE-nohs), or peasant farmers. The rest taught in the cities. In about five months, over 406,000 Nicaraguans learned to read and write.

Because most of the children who volunteered had never experienced life outside the city, the effort became a kind of cultural exchange. *Brigadistas* carried backpacks full of everything they might need. They were sent to homes that were generally several miles apart, and each taught a family or two. The city children were often surprised to find that *campesinos* did not know what a television or a car was. In addition to teaching, *brigadistas* were expected to participate in the family's farmwork and household chores. Many later reported that the experience was the most inspiring thing they had ever done.

After the Sandinistas left the government, public education suffered. However, the situation is improving; in 2002 the number of children completing elementary school had risen to 29 percent. More than three-quarters of the children attend school at least for a while, even if they do not complete their education. Parents in Nicaragua place a high importance on education, but it is expensive. Even "free" public schools charge for textbooks as well as a small monthly fee. Many require simple uniforms, but even this is beyond the budget of many families. School may only last a couple of hours a day. Families who can afford the cost will send their children to a private school, where they will receive a better education.

Elementary school graduates who can afford to go on to high school and college, often enter liberal arts programs, but in the past few years, universities have seen an increase in the number of people studying to be doctors, engineers, or scientists. Nicaragua has numerous universities, of which the National Autonomous University of Nicaragua is the country's oldest and largest.

United Nations Educational, Scientific, and Cultural Organization (UNESCO) awarded the Nicaraguan government the 1980 grand prize in literacy. Today the Literacy Crusade is still a cherished accomplishment for Nicaraguans.

RELIGION

ALTHOUGH NICARAGUA has no official religion, the most widely practiced faith is Roman Catholicism. However, Catholicism has declined somewhat in recent years. In the 1960s, over 95 percent of Nicaraguans belonged to the Catholic Church. In 2004 that number decreased to 85 percent. Protestants make up around 12 percent of Nicaragua's population. Only a few of the original indigenous beliefs remain, but superstitions and folk beliefs are common throughout the country.

During the Sandinista revolution, a new concept in religion, called liberation theology, emerged in Nicaragua and other parts of Latin America. Liberation theology teaches that God does not want people to be poor and encourages people to try to change their lives.

INDIGENOUS BELIEFS

The religion of the Nicarao people was similar to that of the Aztecs. They worshiped corn and natural phenomena, such as the sun and rain, and believed in several gods associated with these elements. When they died, their possessions were buried with them because they believed in reincarnation and thought they would need their belongings in the next life. Other indigenous groups also practiced shamanism, a form of magic. A shaman was believed to have special god-given powers to heal the sick. In some villages in eastern Nicaragua, shamans still practice traditional healing and are treated with great respect. Many indigenous peoples still go to shamans to worship their ancestors or to communicate with them. Although most indigenous religions have now disappeared, a few vestiges of their traditions remain. Some celebrations, such as the Dance of the Little Devils in Granada, combine Spanish beliefs and indigenous traditional dances and music. Religious holidays, such as the Fiesta of Saint Jerónimo in Masaya, are accompanied by imagery from the old religions.

Some historians believe that the Nicarao adapted readily to Christianity because the symbol for their god of rain was very similar to the Christian cross.

Opposite: **The Church of La Recolección in the city of León. Its facade features the Mexican baroque style.**

Children attending Sunday school in church.

ROMAN CATHOLICS

Ever since the Spanish brought Roman Catholicism to Nicaragua, the Church has played a significant role in Nicaraguan life. When the Sandinistas overthrew Somoza Debayle, they unravelled the tight knot between the government and religion. Some factions of the Church supported the Sandinistas, while others aided the Contras. Many of the reforms the Sandinistas made were too radical for the conservative bishops in Nicaragua. Overall, the church hierarchy resisted change and questioned the government's authority. With the change of leadership in 1990, a strong bond between Chamorro's administration and the Church emerged.

For centuries, the Catholic Church has tried to maintain a consistent tradition and resist change. For example, until recently, mass was said in Latin even though few people understood it. In Nicaragua, most Catholics believe in God, obey the Ten Commandments, and go to church, but there is also a group of Catholics who think that going to church is not the only way to show one's faith in God. They feel that some aspects of church worship are unnecessarily rigid and they consider themselves Catholics because they live by their interpretation of Catholic morals and values. To them, one of the most important roles of Catholicism is to help others less fortunate than themselves. Often, this means going against tradition, but they believe they are still acting as God wishes them to.

RELIGIOUS FREEDOM

The Sandinistas guaranteed complete religious freedom, protecting the people's right to worship and practice any faith. They also declared that the Catholic Church would be an important part of reconstruction. Later the Vatican objected to the progressive reforms implemented by the Sandinista regime, and Nicaragua became one of the key places where the Church fought against liberation theology. The Sandinistas said they were prepared to hear criticism and would allow the hierarchy to voice its opposition, but that collaboration between the Church and the contras would not be tolerated. In 1986 the government expelled Bishop Pablo Antonio Vega from the country because he lobbied in Washington, D.C., in support of President Reagan's $100 million Contra-aid plan.

The link between religion and politics was especially controversial during the Sandinista years. Many priests were also members of the FSLN, and conservative Catholics opposed this idea, saying that the interests of the Church and the state were in conflict. While the Church and the Sandinistas disagreed on many things, both groups understood the benefits of maintaining a working relationship. In 1986 President Ortega and the highest church official, Cardinal Obando y Bravo, held talks to discuss how to proceed. The Sandinistas believed that if they had Cardinal Obando on their side, the public would also support their efforts.

Cardinal Obando was, and remains, widely respected in Nicaragua. He was appointed head of the National Reconciliation Commission in 1987, formed to improve relations between the government and church leaders. He was also selected to mediate in ceasefire talks with the Contras, but he used this position to help Chamorro get elected. In 2005 Cardinal Obando helped resolve a constitutional crisis sparked by the major political parties fighting for power.

During the Sandinista regime, the Church forced priests who held government positions to either resign from them or give up the priesthood. They also transferred priests who supported the revolution out of poor barrios and into middle-class neighborhoods, where the people were less likely to support their progressive ideas.

PROTESTANT CHURCHES

About 15 percent of Nicaraguans are Protestant or Evangelical. While the Catholic Church is the only religious organization with a strong presence throughout the country, around 118 different non-Catholic faiths are also practiced. Most Nicaraguans who changed their religion did so in the 1970s. They were unhappy the Catholic Church in Nicaragua had strongly supported the Somoza regime. As the revolution began to build, the poor started to reject Catholicism. The largest Evangelical congregation, the Moravian, has many non-mestizo members from the Mosquito Coast.

The Moravian Church, originally from Germany, was the first Protestant group to gain a foothold in historically Catholic Nicaragua. The Moravians sent missionaries to Bluefields in 1849, and today they are a very important religious influence across the country's Atlantic coast. In the early 1900s the rest of Nicaragua was exposed to Protestantism when interdenominational groups from the United States began to send missionaries. In the 1970s some Nicaraguans came to believe that the Catholic Church, which had been introduced by Spanish conquerors, was ignoring the plight of Nicaragua's poor. They felt it was more concerned with supporting whichever government was in power. Numerous Nicaraguans gradually turned toward Protestant denominations. During the 1970s and 1980s, hundreds of thousands left the Catholic Church. When foreign missionaries began to turn leadership over to Nicaraguans, especially in the 1990s, even more people converted to Protestantism.

The largest Protestant group in Nicaragua is the Assemblies of God, a Pentecostal denomination. Up to 85 percent of the Protestant churches in Nicaragua are Pentecostal. Pentecostals are Christians who believe that God's spirit can enter them and help them heal sick people or even make them speak a language they do not know. In many poor, urban neighborhoods,

Pentecostals make up more than 50 percent of the population. Baptist, Seventh-Day Adventist, and nondenominational churches are also important in some areas. These Protestant churches are very small and completely independent, unlike Catholic churches, which are all under the same leadership. Perhaps because they are relatively new, Protestant churches seem to have better attendance than the Catholic ones; there are probably more Protestants in church on Sunday morning than Catholics.

THE POPULAR CHURCH

In the late 1960s, Roman Catholic priests from all over Latin America met in Colombia to discuss liberation theology, a concept based on the idea that God does not want people to be poor or to be treated badly. Until that time, most Roman Catholics believed poverty and injustice existed because God created them. Poor people assumed their fate was God's will and nothing they did could change it.

Nicaraguan children find church a comfortable and familiar place to meet friends.

The priests who believed in liberation theology taught the poor to take an active role in changing their lives to break free from the cycle of poverty. This progressive movement became known as the Popular Church. Two of its early members were the poet-priest Ernesto Cardenal, who became the minister of culture during the Sandinista regime, and his brother Fernando, who became minister of education and headed the 1980 Literacy Crusade. Priests of the Popular Church made their church services more appealing to the common people by saying Mass in Spanish and by discussing solutions to common problems. Catholic Church leaders opposed the Popular Church movement because they believed people should accept their station in life as God's will.

Nicaraguans are religious
people but generally do
not frown on gambling,
drinking, or promiscuity.

RELIGION IN PRACTICE

Nicaraguans have a lot of faith in God, but they are often suspicious of priests. The country has a long history of anticlericalism, or lack of faith in the clergy. One reason for this is that many of the high officials in the Catholic Church and even some of the local priests have been rather wealthy. Sometimes they were landlords (some still are) who profited at the expense of the poor. People who believe that a good Christian should help out the less fortunate have trouble accepting the Church's opposition to social development programs intended to help the poor.

Roger Lancaster, an anthropologist who lived in Nicaragua for several years, observed that Nicaraguans are highly religious, but not very pious. They are devoted to certain religious beliefs, but at the same time they do not follow all the dogmatic rituals that make a person devout. Lancaster noted that not as many Nicaraguans attend church regularly as he had expected, and that cursing, drinking, gambling, promiscuity, and other activities considered sinful by the church are common among Nicaraguans.

In a conversation with a 22-year-old Nicaraguan man named Elvis, Lancaster found an explanation for this discrepancy between theory and practice. "I believe in God, in my own way," Elvis said. "I believe in right living and worshiping God by doing right. Be humble, be honest, don't exploit people." It seems that people in Elvis's country have many different ideas about what is the right way to live, but somehow they all manage to make their various ways of life fit in with their belief in God.

CITY OF GOD

In the mid-1970s, a Catholic sect called the Word of God, which is based in Ann Arbor, Michigan, founded a branch called the City of God in Managua. Members of this sect believe that injustice is divinely dictated and that they have been chosen by God to carry out His will. Their lives revolve around trying to find God and to achieve personal communication with Him. Sometimes this leads to visions and mystical revelations. Members of the group believe their leaders have great authority because God has spoken to them and told them how to lead their followers.

The City of God sect, still very strong in Nicaragua in 2005, had an interesting connection to the government in the 1980s, which led to the construction of Managua's cathedral. A leader of the City of God, Carlos Mántica, was a close friend of President Chamorro, and four members of her cabinet also belonged to the sect. A prominent member of the Word of God was American business tycoon Thomas Monaghan, the founder of Domino's Pizza, who was on the committee responsible for building the new cathedral in Managua (a committee headed by Chamorro herself). He paid for most of the $3 million in construction costs for the cathedral.

CHURCHES

The city of Granada is the best place in Nicaragua to see beautiful churches. Besides the splendid cathedral (*right*), three other old churches are located here: the Chapel of Maria Auxiliadora, La Merced, and Jalteva. León is the home of an enormous cathedral—one which was intended for Lima and mistakenly built in León— elaborately decorated with many fine statues in ivory, bronze, and silver. The tomb of Rubén Darío, Nicaragua's most famous poet, is also located here.

The oldest church in Nicaragua, the parish church of Subtiava, is located in León. The cathedral in Subtiava has a unique feature: a bright yellow sun with a smiling face is painted on the ceiling. When the Spaniards built the cathedral, they included this feature because they thought this would encourage the indigenous people to come to church, as they worshiped a sun god. The Spanish priests hoped to convert the indigenous people to Christianity once they were in the church.

FOLK BELIEFS AND SUPERSTITION

While educated, urban Nicaraguans have few superstitions, certain interesting notions are common in the countryside and among the poor due to Nicaragua's long tradition of rural folk culture. Many mestizos who live in western Nicaragua believe that blacks along the east coast practice witchcraft. While black magic and the evil eye are associated almost exclusively with people living on the "other" side, some Nicaraguan men believe all women have the power to cast spells over them. Women are said to know how to enchant and bewitch men into liking them, although few men, if any, have witnessed such a spell being cast.

The tradition seems to be perpetuated by its own built-in factor of secrecy. Women never admit to knowing witchcraft but do not deny it either. Men think mothers teach their daughters how to cast spells and forbid them from ever telling the men about it. In this way, the men are kept wondering if witchcraft exists. The most common spell is the cigar spell. If a woman wants to make her wandering husband come back to her, she should chant a certain incantation over the smoke of a cigar that she must light at midnight.

Other stories and legends from the western region indicate belief in ghosts, devils, and evil spirits. Some people believe that when a mother dies, her soul remains on earth to watch over her children. Her spirit is said to roam the land of the living until all her children have grown old and passed on. The story of Segua, an enchanted woman who roams at night and makes a low whistling sound, is often associated with curses and spells. Nicaraguans believe that anyone who sees Segua might have a change of luck. Another popular story tells of people who can change humans into animals because they have sold their souls to the devil. Possession by the devil is usually thought to cause insanity or make people cruel and evil.

A Nicaraguan woman casts a cigar spell which is believed to make a roaming husband return.

In eastern coastal communities, folklore is more likely to involve nature and animals. A Miskito legend explains the seasons by personifying summer and winter as two people arguing over whether sun or rain is better for the land. Winter suggests they take turns demonstrating their powers to decide. Summer makes everything too hot and dry, killing plants, animals, and people. Winter creates rain, then has to stop for a while to let the rain dry up. In the end, the seasons decide to take turns working and resting so there will be a correct balance of rain and heat.

LANGUAGE

NICARAGUANS LOVE TO TALK, and it seems they always have something to say. The official language is Spanish, but a few indigenous languages have survived among the Miskitos, Ramas, and Sumos living along the eastern coast. Western aboriginal languages have all but disappeared, but their influence is still seen in place names and nouns in Nicaraguan Spanish. Many streets, schools, buildings, and neighborhoods are also named after famous Nicaraguans, especially revolutionary heroes and martyrs. The dialect of Spanish spoken in Nicaragua is characterized by interesting expressions, unique pronunciations, and the inclusion of indigenous and English words.

Above: **Mothers of Sandinista war heroes display their own language of love in a demonstration against fighting.**

Opposite: **A food vendor in the northern city of Estelí advertises her menu on the walls of her stall.**

NICARAGUAN SPANISH

The language Nicaraguans speak today is a blend of Spanish, indigenous, and Nicaraguan words. The various indigenous groups spoke many different languages. Most of these became obsolete after the Spaniards arrived and taught their language to the indigenous people. Miskito and other indigenous languages were combined with Spanish, but eventually most people spoke Spanish.

When the Spaniards encountered things for which their language had no words, they adapted the indigenous names but often pronounced them in a slightly different way. That is one reason why Nicaraguan Spanish is a little different from the Spanish spoken in Spain and other Latin American countries. Also, most urban Nicaraguans include some English words and expressions that they picked up from North American music or movies. For example, young Nicaraguans say "I love you" in English, and the popular words for money are the English "money" and "cash."

93

PRONUNCIATION

Nicaraguans speak rather carelessly, often ignoring grammar rules and shortening words or phrases. They almost always drop the *s* sound from the end of words pronounced with an *s* by people in Spain. The often-used expression *"va pues,"* pronounced "bah PWE," is one example. The term does not really mean anything: it is like saying "All right, then." Nicas say it all the time. When they momentarily have nothing to say, they say *"Si pues"* (see PWE), or "Yes, then."

Another interesting characteristic of Nicaraguan Spanish is the number of words that mean "machete." A machete is a big, long blade, much like a short sword. It is only sharp on one side, and is often used for cutting a path through heavy vegetation. If Eskimos have a hundred words for snow, the Nicaraguans have a hundred related to the machete. One of them, *machetazo* (mah-sheh-TAH-zoh), describes someone who gets sliced up by someone else wielding a machete.

As Spanish is spoken across Latin America, and Central America occupies a small area geographically, there are few terms that are unique to Nicaragua. Below are some words that are characteristic of casual Nicaraguan Spanish.

English	Nicaraguan	Pronunciation
What's going on?/What's up?	*Ideay*	eee-dee-EYE
to embarrass someone	*achantar*	ah-CHAN-tahr
awful	*chocho*	CHOH-choh
leave a place/go straight/ go on a trip	*va de viaje*	vah deh vee-AH-hey
boy/girl	*chavalo/chavala*	cha-VAL-oh/cha-VAL-ah

EXPRESSIONS

Nicaraguan Spanish is full of expressions and idioms. "Walking with the avocados" describes someone who has his or her head in the clouds. Someone who brags a lot is said to think he or she is "Tarzan's mother." Someone stupid and irritating is called *baboso* (bah-BOH-soh), which means something like slimy slug in English. When people are disgusted, they might exclaim, "*¡Qué barbaridad!*" (KEH bar-bar-ee-DAHD; how barbaric).

Two very common expressions used during the difficult and shortage-plagued 1980s were *no hay* (noh-EYE), which means there is none, and *la vida es dura* (lah BEE-dah ehs DOO-rah), which means life is hard.

The term *búfalo* (BOO-fah-loh, or buffalo) describes someone or something strong and robust. If Nicaraguans say someone has a good coconut, it means he or she is smart, and a dunce is called a *burro* (BOO-roh, or donkey). Names of fruit are often used in sexual metaphors; for example, a handsome fellow is called a mango. Someone who cannot make up his or her mind is called *gallo-gallina* (GUY-oh-gah-YEE-nah, or rooster-hen). Children are affectionately referred to as *monos*, or monkeys.

There are several proverbs that express the idea that everyone has a bout of bad luck once in a while. One such proverb is "Even the best monkey occasionally drops a zapote." (A zapote is a tropical fruit.)

The Nicaraguan saying "Every pig has its Saturday" refers to the inevitable occasional streak of bad luck. It has its origin in the practice of preparing pork on Saturday for a special meal on Sunday.

There are many parts to a married woman's name. In the above example, Anita is the first name, Santiago is her father's family name, and Obando is her husband's family name, preceded by the word "de."

NAMES AND TITLES

It is a custom to address people older than one with the respectful title *Don* (DAHN) or *Doña* (DAH-nyah). These words derive from the archaic Spanish words for lord and lady. They are formal titles like sir and madam, but they could also be interpreted as Mr. and Mrs. Traditionally, *Don* and *Doña* were also used when speaking to people of a higher social class, and such people were not obliged to return the courtesy. After the revolution, people started to use more informal terms.

Many people also address someone who has published poetry with the title *Poeta* (poh-EH-tah). While it is not a formal title, Nicaraguans often use it because they like to treat poets with respect.

In Nicaragua, English first names are common. Spanish names can be tricky to understand because there are different formulas for men's and women's names. Men put their mother's family name at the end of their names, while women drop their mother's name when they get married and add their husband's. For example, former president Ortega's full name is Daniel Ortega Saavedra—his first name is Daniel, his father's name is Ortega, and his mother's maiden name is Saavedra. An example of a married woman's name is Violeta Barrios de Chamorro. Her first name is Violeta, her father's family name is Barrios, and when she married Pedro Joaquín Chamorro Cardenal, she added his father's family name to the end of her own, prefaced by the small word de. Violeta's mother's name is no longer part of Violeta's name.

It becomes even more confusing when someone has two first names, like Pedro Joaquín. Speaking informally, people refer to him as simply Pedro Joaquín.

LOCAL DIALECTS

Early indigenous people communicated by writing hieroglyphics, or symbols that conveyed messages or stories, on special paper made from tree bark.

The native languages of the indigenous groups in eastern Nicaragua shared the linguistic pattern of the

Hieroglyphics of early Indians.

Chibcha group of northern South American natives. Indigenous people in the west, such as the Nicarao, spoke languages derived from the Nahuatl linguistic family. Nahuatl languages include those of the Maya and Aztecs, and other Mexican and southern North American indigenous groups. Indigenous groups in western Nicaragua found it necessary and practical to speak Spanish, giving up their native tongues. By the mid-19th century, only a few people still spoke indigenous languages there.

On the eastern coast, some indigenous people still speak their native languages. The main dialect is Miskito, and some of its words are English. Since the Miskitos have no words for numbers over 10, for instance, they use the English words. They also have a custom of naming their children after whatever they see around them at the time of birth. There is supposedly a man living in Zelaya whose name is General Electric. Some Miskito words are *tingki-pali*, or thank you very much, and *nakis-ma*, which means how are you? English is the primary language of most people of African origin in the region, but Creole—a mixture of English, Spanish, aboriginal, and black Carib languages—is also quite common.

ARTS

NICARAGUA HAS A STRONG literary tradition and is perhaps best known as the birthplace of Rubén Darío, its most famous poet. Poetry is extremely popular, and many Nicaraguans have achieved fame for their writing. The visual and performing arts are appreciated on a local level but have yet to gain international acclaim. Perhaps the most important element of art in Nicaraguan culture is folk art—the paintings, drawings, music, and crafts created by ordinary people. This tradition began long before Columbus sailed to Central America and is shared by most cultures in the region.

RUBÉN DARÍO

Nicaragua has produced more poets than any other Latin American country. The most famous is Rubén Darío, leader of the modernist movement that freed traditional Latin American writing from European rules. Darío's vision influenced Nicaraguan writing as well as all of Latin American literature.

Darío was fond of Walt Whitman, Edgar Allan Poe, and the French Parnassians and symbolists. His poetry was based on ordinary objects, but he used his imagination to elevate common experiences. Much of his early verse described the beauty of the Nicaraguan landscape—the flaming sun, the farms, the pigs, and chickens. Darío's poems often associated artistic and spiritual values with Latin America, and materialism and false values with North America. Nevertheless, American *New York Times* correspondent Stephen Kinzer, described reading Darío as his "most magical and most unexpected" adventure during 13 years of covering Nicaragua.

In Managua, the performing arts center is named after Darío, and the highest national honor for poetry also bears his name. Metapa, the neighborhood in Matagalpa where he was born in 1867, is now called Ciudad Darío as a symbol of respect.

Above: **Monument to Rubén Darío.**

Opposite: **A Nicaraguan potter creating jugs at his potter's wheel.**

Ernesto Cardenal, a priest, poet, and minister of culture during the Sandinista years.

OTHER WELL-KNOWN WRITERS

Almost everyone in Nicaragua has tried their hand at writing poetry, including former president Ortega. Much of the poetry written in this century reflects the atmosphere of oppression, injustice, and fear that has been present in Nicaragua for decades.

In the past two decades, many women have begun publishing poetry. Before the revolution, most popular poets were men, and their poetry was often political. Much of the poetry written by women has more to do with love, nature, and beauty beyond the material world.

The Literary Vanguard, established in 1927, was a group of writers inspired by Sandino's determination to drive U.S. Marines out of Nicaragua. The Vanguard's goal was the liberation of Nicaraguan literature from foreign domination, to encourage the growth of native literature.

Joaquín Pasos (1914–47) was an early member of the Vanguard. His poetry is filled with images of thought and emotion that reflect the character of life in Nicaragua. Another *vanguardista* (bahn-gwar-DEE-tah) was Pablo Antonio Cuadra (1912–2002), a popular author who wrote about everyday life in free verse. He knew Sandino in his youth, and his many poems dealing with political injustice show the strong impression Sandino's ideas left on him. Cuadra also wrote several delightful and brilliant pieces about nature. A versatile writer, Cuadra wrote a drama in 1937, several years before modern theater came to Nicaragua.

Since the 1940s, another great poet, Ernesto Cardenal (1925–), has written poems that are probably the most widely read in the Spanish language today. Cardenal, also a priest, was appointed minister of culture during the Sandinista years. His early poems were about his love of women, but his more recent poems speak of the beauty of natural things and the wonders and cruelties of urban life. The short stores of Sergio Ramírez (1942–) contain characters living uniquely Nicaraguan lives, such as a baseball player who faces execution as a political prisoner. Ramírez published a novel in 1988, *Castigo divino* (Divine Justice), that dramatizes a series of uprisings from 1930 to 1961; it is a carefully woven portrait of the nation's troubles. Other famous writers include poets Santiago Argüello (1872–1940) and Gioconda Belli (1948–) and novelist Hernán Robleto (1892–1969), author of *Sangre en el Trópico* (Blood In The Tropics).

The elegant Rubén Darío National Theater in Managua is named after Nicaragua's most famous poet.

THEATER

Theater is an important form of artistic expression in Nicaragua. The National Theater School, a teaching facility, presents performances by students. Another small theater, the Justo Rufino Garay Theater Hall, offers drama by professional troupes from all over Latin America. It is also home to one of Nicaragua's most exciting and adventurous theater companies, the El Grupo de Teatro Justo Rufino Garay. The Rubén Darío National Theater hosts leading international productions.

"At the beginning I had no idea there was a market for paintings like these, but now we can't turn out enough to meet the demand."

—Maria Silva, a Nicaraguan painter

PAINTING AND SCULPTURE

Some important Nicaraguan artists include the sculptor Genaro Amador Lira and Asilia Guillén, a painter best known for her *Las Isletas*, a beautiful landscape of the islands in Lake

Guillén lived for a time at the Solentiname art colony, where she became friends with Ernesto Cardenal, the poet-priest who helped establish the colony. Cardenal brought paint, canvas, and brushes to Solentiname for the first time and encouraged residents to paint what they saw around them. About a dozen talented painters, mostly women, emerged from the colony. Their paintings are primitive and bright. Some have political themes, while others are beautiful landscapes and depictions of the richness of tropical life.

ARTS AND CRAFTS

The tradition of folk art began with the pottery, baskets, and weaving of the indigenous people long before the Spanish arrived. The Nicarao people created many fine ceramics, metal ornaments, and carved stones. They were known for their skill and imagination in carving jade and other precious and semiprecious stones. The Nicarao traded some of these wares in markets where the standard of exchange was usually cacao. Throughout Mexico and Central America, the indigenous peoples produced a variety of crafts, but only a few artifacts have survived.

Today's arts and crafts are often made by people who have learned the ancient methods passed down from generation to generation. Thus, it is still possible to see how the early indigenous people might have used their skills and resources. For example, several indigenous groups practiced loom-weaving using cotton thread colored with natural dyes made from plants and minerals. They used coal to make black dye, blackberry fruits for blue, achiote seeds from the annatto tree for red, and clay for yellow. The hardest color to obtain was purple, which came from an insect living on cactus plants. Today indigenous peoples use synthetic dyes, but they still weave traditional patterns.

Nicaragua has a ceramics tradition that dates back to the time of the Nicarao people.

Another craft that has been around for a long time is macramé, a way of knotting strings or ropes to make decorative designs. The hammock was also created by the indigenous people, who used little other furniture. Two museums, the National Museum in Managua and the Tenderi Museum of Indian Artifacts in Masaya, maintain significant collections of folk and indigenous art, as well as a few pre-Columbian objects.

Dancing and music are very important parts of folk culture. Street performers can be seen in all the major cities, especially Managua. They dress up in elaborate masks and bright costumes to dance, play music, and entertain audiences with skits or songs.

THE NEW FOLK ART

A recent development in the world of Nicaraguan art is mural painting. Murals are large-scale visual stories painted directly on walls, often created by several people working together. Some art experts say that Nicaragua may soon become the world capital of mural art.

Many of the murals in Nicaragua were painted by young people who wanted to express how they felt about their country's political affairs. In fact, most murals portray political messages or stories of historical events that have had a strong influence on Nicaraguans. Try to picture what some of the murals look like:

- A mural covering the exterior walls of a children's library in Managua symbolizes the difference between life under the Somoza regime and life with the Sandinistas in power. One side, painted with dark, cloudy colors, shows children breaking a heavy steel chain that surrounds a high bookshelf covered with dust and cobwebs. The children are reaching up to grab the few books that fall down. The other half of the mural uses bright, happy hues to show children selecting books from an easily reachable shelf and reading them at a large table.
- Another mural shows a woman carrying the blue-and-white flag of Nicaragua and walking next to a man carrying the red-and-black flag of the Sandinista party. It was painted in Granada in the 1980s.
- The largest mural in the country, covering a wall along an entire city block in Managua, represents a series of events in Nicaraguan history.

FOLK MUSIC

While Nicaraguans appreciate many types of music, the traditional sounds of folk music are some of the most appealing. The typical Nicaraguan musical genre is called *Son Nica* (sohn NEE-ca) and usually contains driving rhythms along with good instrumentals. The Ritchie Valens tune *La Bamba*—or the Los Lobos rendition—gives a pretty good idea of what Nicaraguan music sounds like. Along the eastern coast, *costeña* (koh-STEH-nyah) music is very popular. It is a combination of reggae and calypso.

Some special instruments are used to produce the unique rhythms and melodies of folk music. The *marimba* (mah-REEM-bah) is like a xylophone, but is made of special wood. It has been around for centuries and is still the most popular instrument in folk music. Other pre-Columbian instruments include *maracas* (mah-RAH-kahs), gourds that are dried so the seeds inside produce a rattling sound. The *chirimia* (chehr-MEE-yah) is a woodwind instrument similar to a clarinet.

The marimba is the most popular instrument of Nicaraguan folk musicians.

LEISURE

IN THEIR FREE TIME, Nicaraguans like to relax and have fun with their friends. Sports events, especially baseball games, always attract crowds of spectators. People do not just like to watch; they also like to play baseball, soccer, and other sports. When the weather is really hot, families often go to the beach to cool off in the water and have a picnic lunch. But perhaps the favorite pastime is lounging at home. Nicaraguans love to talk, tell stories, and reminisce. Sometimes they watch television, but more often they just sit on the front porch and chat with neighbors.

BASEBALL—THE NATIONAL SPORT

In most Latin American countries, soccer and bullfighting are the most popular sports, but in Nicaragua the national sport is beisbol (BAYZ-bohl), or baseball. The game was introduced to the country by U.S. Marines in the 1930s, and it soon became more popular than soccer.

Over 200 teams compete at the local and regional levels, and the best ones play in the national championship games. Most cities have baseball stadiums, where people go to watch their home team play. The largest one, in Managua, holds 40,000 people. But the biggest baseball heroes are Nicaraguans who have made it to the U.S. major leagues: Vincent Padilla, Marvin Bernard, and many others.

Little boys learn to play baseball by the time they are 4 or 5. Girls play too, but often prefer basketball or volleyball. Children's baseball games take place in fields, parks, vacant lots, or on the streets. Most of them have figured out that a stick works just as well as a bat. Some simply use their forearms to hit the ball. No pitcher is needed when they play this way; the batter just throws the ball up and hits it when it comes down. Some children are lucky enough to have a tennis ball to substitute for a baseball, but most use one made out of rags wrapped tightly around a small rock.

On July 28, 1991, Nicaraguan Dennis "El President" Martinez, playing for the Montreal Expos, became the first Latin American major league baseball player to pitch a perfect game. It is said that on this day, the Contras and the Sandinistas set aside their differences to celebrate the historical moment.

Opposite: **Baseball is Nicaragua's favorite sport, as evidenced by this group of men playing the game on Ometepe Island.**

BASEBALL GIVES A BOY HOPE

A motorcycle crash that almost led to the amputation of his right leg did not stop one young Nicaraguan from returning to his love: playing baseball. Like many Nicaraguan boys (*right*), Sandor Guido let the love of baseball help him through the hard times. Guido began playing at a young age, and by the time he was 15 he was playing for one of the best leagues in Nicaragua.

In late 1998, when Guido was 20, a tire blew on the motorcycle he was riding. It crashed into a fence and he suffered serious injuries to his right leg. Many thought he would never play baseball again. But after two months in the hospital and additional therapy in the United States, doctors offered him hope that he could recover, and he began to dream of playing baseball again. Recovery took several months and was a painful ordeal, but he persevered and started playing not only baseball again, but basketball, too.

Today he is one of the hot young prospects of Nicaraguan baseball, and he is among the León team's best fielders. He also has a degree in dentistry, specializing in orthodontics. While Guido says that he may not run as fast as before, he has finally succeeded in achieving his dream of playing for the Nicaraguan national baseball team.

OTHER POPULAR SPORTS

After baseball, the next favorite sport is most likely soccer. This game was very popular with Europeans, who probably introduced the sport into Nicaragua in the 19th century. Teams for men, women, and children are organized in cities, towns, and villages.

Basketball and volleyball are two other common recreational sports, and many cities have established teams for adults who enjoy a little friendly competition. Junior basketball and volleyball leagues are growing fast because more young people are becoming interested in these sports. Track and field and martial arts are not as common, but are relatively

popular. Boxing is quite popular, especially after the success of Managua-born Ricardo "El Matador" Mayorga, who won the World Boxing Association (WBA)/World Boxing Championship (WBC) welterweight title in 2002–03. Wealthy people like to play tennis and go sailing. The equipment needed for these sports costs a lot to buy or rent, and most people cannot afford such amusements.

Two popular spectator sports are bullfighting and cockfighting. In rural villages and along the eastern coast, farmers bring their roosters to a clearing where they pit the birds against each other and place bets on which one will win. Roosters have a natural drive to defend their territory, and some people find it entertaining to watch them attack each other. Bullfighting is a traditional Spanish activity that is often part of festivals and celebrations. In Spain, the object of a bullfight is for the matador (the person fighting the bull) to kill the animal, but in Nicaragua the matador has to try to mount and ride the bull. He is judged not only on ability, but also on his style.

More basketball leagues are being formed as the game gains popularity among young people.

Above: **A woman relaxes in a rocking chair while the children play nearby.**

Opposite: **Talking on the telephone is a special treat, because few homes have telephones. Every neighborhood usually has a public telephone, but callers just have to hope that whoever answers will be able to track down the person they want to talk to.**

A PLACE TO SOCIALIZE

When they are not playing or watching sports, Nicaraguans enjoy just hanging around with their family and friends. In many neighborhoods, people leave their front door open all day so they can call out greetings to passers-by and invite them in for a cold drink. Most homes have front porches where people gather in the evenings to talk, tell stories, and listen to the radio. When it is really hot, everyone takes a chair out to the porch, faces it inward, and watches television from there. Almost all families have a set of rocking chairs—big ones for adults and little ones for kids. Family time is spent on the porch or in the living room relaxing in their rockers. The chairs can be made of carved wood or woven bamboo.

FAVORITE PASTIMES

Almost every home in Nicaragua has at least one radio. In fact, for every four people, there is one radio. In the United States, there are two radios for each person. Nicaraguans listen to music, news, and a variety of political-discussion programs while they do chores around the house and during their free time. In the evenings, some stations broadcast made-for-radio mysteries or soap operas. Many shows from other countries can also be heard on Nicaraguan radio.

There are not as many homes with television sets in Nicaragua as there are in more developed countries, but people who do not own one usually have relatives or neighbors who do. At 7 P.M. on weekdays nearly everyone in the country is seated in front of the television for the *novela* (noh-VEH-

STORYTELLING

Nicaraguans love to tell jokes, stories, and limericks. Before the revolution, less than half of the population could read or write, so few stories were recorded on paper. Now writers have compiled volumes of stories and fairytales, but many people still know some of them by heart.

Sukling Kwakwalhra (*The Proud Toad*) is an old Miskito fable. It is the story of a toad who wanted to go to a party that the buzzards were throwing at their house in the clouds. All the birds were invited, and the toad was determined to join them. He stopped a hawk who was getting ready to leave for the party. "I'm going too," the toad said, "but I'm going to arrive a little later. Would you be kind enough to carry this bag up to the buzzards' house? My bamboo flute is in the bag, and I would like to play it to make the party festive." The hawk agreed. The toad jumped into the bag, unseen by the hawk, and was carried swiftly up to the party in the clouds. There the toad played the flute all night long. "Ruku, ruku, ruku," the song went. When the party ended, the toad was too proud to ask the birds to take him back down to earth. He jumped into the bag, hoping the hawk would remember the flute. The hawk forgot, however, and the buzzards threw the bag out when they cleaned up after the party. The toad fell down, down, down, until he landed—splat—on a rock. That, the story goes, is why all toads are flat. When the sky is cloudy, Nicaraguans say, you can hear the toads sing, "Ruku, ruku, ruku" for the sun to come out again so the buzzards will have another party.

lah) or soap opera, which is so widely watched that evening meetings are never scheduled for that hour. In the cities, cable television is available, and many of the networks that people enjoy in the United States are shown with Spanish dubbing or subtitles. There are also a few nationwide channels that broadcast to anyone with an antenna. Children love to watch cartoons like *Spongebob Squarepants* and *Yu-gi-oh!* Other favorites are music videos, talk shows, and old American movies.

Few people can afford to go to the movies often, but when they have a little extra money, films are a big hit. Even poor families go once in a while as a special treat. All the major cities have movie theaters that show films, mainly from the United States, in English with Spanish subtitles. Occasionally, a Nicaraguan-made film will appear, usually at one of a few museum theaters. A movie ticket typically costs the equivalent of $4.

Going to the beach to swim, surf, or have a picnic is often a family affair.

A DAY AT THE BEACH

January to April—when the sun beats down hard almost every day and temperatures rise above 100°F (38°C)—is beach season. Nicaraguans head for nearby beaches on weekends and holidays to relax, swim, and have picnics. From Managua, it is an hour-long bus ride to one of several beaches. The most popular ones include Pochomil and Masachapa, located side by side on the Pacific Ocean. One of the most beautiful beaches is El Velero, northwest of Managua. The sea there is great for surfing and swimming, but it costs the equivalent of $6 to enter, so it is more popular with upper-class families and tourists.

Although Lake Managua, Lake Nicaragua, and several smaller lakes do not have pretty, sandy beaches, they do offer other interesting activities. Visitors go to the lakes to row or see the volcanoes, but as the water is

A BAVARIAN HIDEAWAY IN THE HIGHLANDS

Although a trip to the beach is the most common form of out-of-town recreation for Nicaraguans, many middle-class Nicaraguans like to escape to the mountains for relaxing and hiking. One such mountain hideaway is the Selva Negra, built by third- and fourth-generation German immigrants. The resort owners' German ancestors were traveling across Nicaragua on their way to California during the 1850s when they decided to stay in Nicaragua and grow coffee. (Nicaragua was used by thousands of people as a short-cut to California during the gold rush.)

Selva Negra is known for its sustainable and environmentally friendly method of farming coffee. The owners of the hacienda (farm) grow coffee in the shade of tall trees as it would have grown in its natural environment. This encourages dozens of species of tropical birds, including the rare three-wattled bellbird, to roost in the trees. Vacationers can choose from any of 14 hiking trails and several horseback riding trails that will take them into the forest to see the birds, ferns, wild orchids, and the trees of the cloud forest.

Selva Negra also practices self-sufficiency and recycling. The food served at the resort is cultivated at the hacienda. The vegetables served at the table are grown organically, that is, no chemicals and pesticides are used, and fertilized with waste products from the animals on the hacienda. These animals, which include cattle and fowl, provide meat, dairy products, and eggs.

polluted in some places, swimming is not a good idea. Usually there are playgrounds, ice-cream stands, and historical landmarks near the lakes.

Not far from Lake Managua, at Acahualinca, is Nicaragua's most significant archaeological artifact. In the 19th century, ancient footprints were discovered in a patch of dried mud that had been preserved by a thick layer of volcanic rock and ash. The footprints were made more than 6,000 years ago by men, women, and animals, including a deer and possibly a jaguar. They head toward the lake; it was initially believed that these people were fleeing an erupting volcano, but that has since been disproved. Instead, tests have shown that they were walking at normal speed and were carrying either a heavy load of supplies or children.

FESTIVALS

THROUGHOUT THE YEAR, Nicaraguans celebrate many holidays with parades, grand fiestas, elaborate meals, and religious ceremonies. Music and dancing make these events particularly enjoyable. One of the largest festivals is Masaya's Carnaval, or the Festival of Disguises, when people dress up in elaborate costumes to attend balls, banquets, and parades, and to listen to speeches. Carnaval provides a forum for people who do not agree with popular ideas and values to speak out about their beliefs, to dress and act as they please, and to break social rules without getting into trouble. For some people Carnaval means dressing up in disguises, but for others it is a chance to be themselves without fear of criticism. This makes Carnaval a unique Nicaraguan holiday.

Some holidays are religious, such as Purísima and Easter. Some are anniversaries of historical events. Whatever the cause for celebration, Nicaraguans know how to relax and have a good time.

Above: **Masks add to the festive mood of Carnaval.**

Opposite: **Masked dancers in costume perform at the Carnaval in Masaya.**

CALENDAR OF FESTIVALS

Week before Easter	Semana Santa	November 1	All Saints' Day
March/April	Pascua (Easter)	November 2	All Souls' Day
July 19	Anniversary of Sandinista Revolution	December 7	Purísima (Immaculate Conception)
August 1–10	Santo Domingo (in Managua)	December 25	Navidad (Christmas)
September 15	Independence Day		

PURÍSIMA

One of the most important Roman Catholic holidays in Nicaragua is Purísima, also called Gritería, a celebration of the Virgin Mary. In most areas, it is celebrated on December 7, but in Managua the holiday involves a week of festivities, ending with a huge festival on December 7. It is believed the tradition of celebrating Purísima originated centuries ago when the Cerro Negro volcano erupted. It spilled lava for days and the people in nearby León feared that it would never stop. Then one day, they placed a statue of the Virgin Mary on the smoldering ground near the volcano and the volcano soon became still. The people believed that the Virgin Mary had stopped the volcano and saved them from further harm.

Preparations for this holiday begin weeks in advance with several families in each neighborhood setting up elaborate altars to the Virgin Mary. They invite friends and relatives over on the evening of December 6 to see the altars and sing hymns in Mary's honor. The altars are draped in fabric and decorated with lights, candles, flowers, branches, and leaves. Each one features an image of the Virgin Mary. Chairs are set up so visitors can stop and pray at the altar. Often, the host gives each guest a cold drink, a piece of sugarcane, a small gift, and an orange or lime before they leave. Because it can be expensive to set up these displays and host large numbers of guests, people take turns at being host, and those who have altars one year are usually guests at friends' homes the following year.

In Managua, the celebration includes an impressive fireworks display on December 7. A big festival is held in some cities, and crowds gather around professionally built altars to sing. Some families eat big feasts of roast pork and traditional Nicaraguan dishes.

The origin of Purísima lies in the eruption of Cerro Negro volcano (above) centuries ago. Purísima fun involves giving away colorful paper baskets filled with candy. Children go from house to house on December 7 shouting, "What brings us so much happiness?" The host shouts back, "The immaculate conception of Mary!" and gives each child a basket. No wonder December 7 is called La Gritería, or the shouting.

OTHER RELIGIOUS HOLIDAYS

In some cities, like León, Purísima is the biggest holiday, but Christmas and Easter are also celebrated with great joy. On Christmas Eve, families sit down to a special meal of chicken or turkey. Some people attend Christmas Eve Mass, and at midnight almost everyone goes out into the street to exchange *abrazos de paz* (ah-VRAH-soh day PAH), or hugs of peace, with friends and neighbors. Christmas trees decorated with lights and ornaments are a common sight, as are bare branches covered with cotton; most homes have some sort of Christmas decoration.

Turkey or chicken is served on Christmas Eve, after which the children look forward to gifts from the God Child or their godparents.

Gift-giving at Christmas is common, but most people have little money to buy presents. Younger children believe in the God Child, a mythical figure who brings gifts, just like Santa Claus. Poor children may not get a gift from their parents or the God Child, but they are almost certain to receive one from their godparents. Even if they cannot afford gifts for their own children, godparents will make sure their godchildren have something to open on Christmas.

Easter, called Pascua in Nicaragua, is usually celebrated by attending church and visiting relatives. The week before Pascua is called Semana Santa, or Holy Week. Activities include processions in honor of the crucifixion. On Good Friday, people show respect for Jesus' suffering by going to church or praying at home. The rest of the week, however, is considered a good time for vacationing.

The holiday falls at the height of the dry season when it is very hot, so much of the population can be found relaxing and playing at the beach. For sports fans, a popular event is the Nicaraguan baseball play-offs, held annually during Semana Santa.

117

People dress up for religious processions and almost everyone in the town or village takes part in one way or another.

SAINTS' DAYS

Another occasion for revelry is the day set aside by each town or village for honoring a patron saint. In Managua, the feast of Saint Dominic is observed over a period of 10 days. From August 1 to August 10, Managuans attend parties, hold parades, and watch bullfights, cockfights, and horse races. The main event is a lively procession as the tiny statue of Saint Dominic is carried from its sanctuary in the southwestern side of town to its temporary home in the old center. The celebration honors Nicaraguans' indigenous heritage as well as their Catholic saint. Church ceremonies commemorate Saint Dominic, but some festival rituals are symbols of the time before the Spanish introduced Catholicism.

The festivals honoring Saint Jerónimo in Masaya and Saint Sebastian in Diriamba are the occasion for folk artists to exhibit their work. Both cities are known for their beautiful indigenous handicrafts. In León, La Merced (Our Lady of Mercy), is a religious holiday. People celebrate by attending church and marching in a procession carrying a large image of La Merced.

On November 1, Nicaraguans throughout the country honor All Saints' Day by going to church and praying to the various saints. The next day is called All Souls' Day, a time to remember the dead. For a week leading up to this day, people go to cemeteries to clean the graves in preparation for All Souls' Day. They also

PUPPETS WITH A PURPOSE

Crowds of excited children and adults gather around *La Gigantona*, or The Giant One, a lavishly decorated, 8-foot (2.4-m) tall puppet dancing in the square. An indigenous tradition that has been around for hundreds of years, *Las Gigantonas* are seen at political rallies, markets, and festivals in Subtiava and other towns. The puppets are created and operated by a troupe of street artists, who travel and perform shows that use humor to criticize the government. Puppets were first used by the indigenous people in León to make fun of the Spaniards. During the war between Somoza and the Sandinistas, *La Gigantona* and her sidekick, a dwarf puppet named Pepe, appeared at anti-Somoza demonstrations.

place flowers on the graves of their loved ones. Often they take something that was special to the dead person, such as a hat, a bottle of the person's favorite drink, or a picture, and leave it on the grave. On the day itself, families take picnic lunches to eat beside their family members' graves. Many spend the day there, visiting other families.

IMPORTANT EVENTS

The oldest national holiday celebrates the day Central American countries became independent from Spain. Independence Day, observed on September 15, brings colorful parades, fireworks, and speeches to the central plaza in most cities. In Granada, this day is celebrated with much fanfare. Schoolchildren and high school drum and bugle corps march through the streets to the plaza, where everyone gathers to listen to speeches by local government officials.

The Sandinista revolution is celebrated on July 19. People from all over Nicaragua take buses to Managua, where a huge rally is held. During the 1980s, the anniversary of the Sandinistas' defeat of Somoza was a popular time for the Sandinista government to speak out about its plans for reform. Now that it is no longer in power, this day has become a time to remember the many people who died during the struggle to defeat Somoza.

Mothers' Day is an important occasion for Nicaraguans. Even people who do not live near their mothers try very hard to visit them on this day. Mothers are sometimes honored by being serenaded early in the morning or at night, after dinner.

FOOD

MEALS IN NICARAGUA range from plain and simple to elaborate and hearty. Nicaraguan dishes are not spicy, unlike Mexican food.

Poverty means that many homes lack food, but people are quite generous with food when they have it. When there is enough money, food can be purchased in a variety of places, and a majority of Nicaraguans also grow some of their own food. Cooking at home is much more common than eating out, even though refrigerators and stoves are not found in every home. Restaurants might serve traditional Nicaraguan dishes along with American-style hamburgers, and a wide selection of ethnic eateries can be found in larger cities.

Above: **A busy outdoor market in Managua, where bargaining over prices is a way of life.**

Opposite: **A Nicaraguan in Bluefields unloads shipments of fruit to be sold at the local market.**

SHOPPING

In any of the western coastal cities of Nicaragua, there is always a supermarket nearby. Imported goods as well as locally produced foods are generally available. Supermarkets also sell cosmetics, clothes, books, stationery, and pots and pans. Shopping for the household is usually a woman's task, although it is also common for mothers to send their children to the market.

For many Nicaraguans, supermarket prices are too high, so they also shop at outdoor markets where vendors sell their goods from individual stalls, and bargaining is common. Many women prefer to shop this way because the produce and meat are fresher than what they can find at a

Some Nicaraguans run general stores, supplying groceries to neighbors.

supermarket. At smaller outdoor markets, vendors walk around with baskets of fruit or other items, and shoppers bargain with vendors over prices until they settle on one that satisfies both parties.

Some markets are held indoors, but the largest ones take up whole blocks of city streets. One of the biggest is the Mercado Oriental in Managua, where vendors are often lined six-deep along sidewalks and streets. Many items found here are black market goods, so they are too expensive for most Nicaraguans. Another important market in Managua is the Mercado Roberto Huembas. At both markets, there are dozens of booths selling staples, such as rice and beans. But some stalls also sell specialized products—one booth at Huembes sells everything that is needed for cake decorating.

Shopping for food at local markets is often a daily requirement because food spoils so quickly in the hot climate. Another place where people get fresh food is at local general stores, which are often located in the converted front rooms of people's houses. Locals know where to go even though most of these stores have no signs. These shops carry staple items and homemade goods, such as tortillas. It is common for people who have refrigerators to buy milk in large amounts and sell it to their neighbors each day. The same goes for people who have ovens—they make tortillas to sell to neighbors who do not have ovens.

SHORTAGES AND HIGH PRICES

Food shortages made life difficult for Nicaraguans during the rule of the Sandinista government. As one Nicaraguan lady says, "Now there is food, and no money to buy it, but in those days, there was no food available to buy." What little food was available at supermarkets was nearly all imported. The price controls set by the government weakened farmers' incentives and caused a drop in local production. The Contra war also took a huge toll on local production. Many farmers were drafted into the national army, reducing the labor force on farms. In addition, the Contras damaged fields of crops, food storage areas, and trucks transporting food to undermine the Sandinistas' efforts to raise the country's standard of living.

Coconut trees are commonly found in the backyards of homes.

By the late 1980s, many thousands of acres of good farm land were abandoned because they were in the war zone. Government attempts at rationing food or subsidizing its cost were ineffective because production had decreased so much. The price of food increased so drastically that by 1988, even the maximum basic salary for a worker supporting a family of six would only buy about 60 percent of what economists call the basic basket of essential products. Families had to have at least two incomes, and even then it was hard to make ends meet. Shortages persisted after the Chamorro administration began in 1990, but since then increased foreign trade and local production have made food less scarce. Today most supermarkets are fully stocked, but people still cannot afford to buy many necessities. One way Nicaraguans cope with this lack of purchasing power is to supplement their diet with food they can rear or grow themselves.

123

A refresco, consumed straight from a plastic pack, makes a refreshing drink on a hot day. Children often sell refrescos on the street or near bus stops, especially in Managua.

COOKING

Like shopping, cooking is usually a woman's job. Nicaraguan specialties often are made using cornmeal. The *nacatamale* (nah-caw-ta-MAL-eh) is considered by many to be Nicaragua's national folk food. It consists of a cornmeal tamale filled with pork, rice, potato, onion, tomato, and green pepper. *Atoles* (ah-TOY-ehs) are deep-fried tortillas with cheese and spices inside. The most traditional dish throughout the country is *gallo pinto* (GUY-oh PEEHN-toh), or painted rooster. It is a mixture of red beans, rice, onions, garlic, and seasonings, all fried in a little oil until crisp. The name comes from the red and white colors of the beans and rice. Most Nicaraguan families eat it at least once a day. Two very common beverages are *refrescos* (ray-FREHS-kohs) and *pinol* (PEEHN-ohl). *Refrescos* are made of fresh fruit juice with a little sugar and water added. Locals can usually tell what flavor the drink is by looking at its color: mango is light orange, papaya is yellow, and tamarind is brown. *Refrescos* are sold with crushed ice in a plastic bag tied at the top. People hold the bag in one hand, bite off a corner, and suck the drink out. *Pinol* is a drink made of toasted ground cornmeal mixed with water or coconut milk and a flavoring like cinnamon or ginger. If it is mixed with some ground cacao, it is called *pinolillo* (peehn-oh-EE-yoh). These beverages are commonly served in a hollowed-out gourd.

Fruits and vegetables are frequently eaten raw or used in preparing a meal. Tomatoes, cabbages, sweet potatoes, avocados, and yucca are common choices. Fruits can be used to make a number of juices, jams, and sauces. Nicaraguans make a wide variety of dishes out of bananas, including porridge, milk shakes, and cakes.

MEALS AND ETIQUETTE

Corn, rice, and beans are staples in every Nicaraguan home. Fortunate families usually have cheese, butter, milk, and tortillas to go with their meals, and once a week or so they have a stew or some other special dish. Less fortunate people might eat only rice and beans. A standard breakfast in a working-class home might consist of two slices of bread with butter (if it is available), an orange or a banana, and heavily sugared coffee. Lunch is usually beans and rice, the leftover bread from breakfast, and maybe a piece of cheese, accompanied by a fruit drink made from lemons or oranges picked from the backyard and sweetened with lots of sugar. Chicken soup may be served instead of beans and rice. A typical dinner consists of *gallo pinto*, tortillas, and fried cheese.

A common practice is the sharing of special food items. When someone in the neighborhood prepares a stew, pasta, roasted meat, or other special meal, she is obligated by social norms and customs to share the food with others in the neighborhood. For example, if a neighbor who stops by to chat while you are cooking "helps" by stirring the pot or throwing in a few spices, she should be given a serving when the meal is ready. Also, whoever lends any vegetables, spices, or other ingredients to the cook is assured a sample of the finished product. Nicaraguans believe that you will have bad luck if others see you being stingy, so you have to share with everyone who saw you fixing a special meal—and anyone who even heard you were serving one.

A neighbor who drops by and happens to stir the pot is entitled to a serving of the food.

HOLIDAY FEASTS

Meals become an elaborate production during holiday seasons. Women begin shopping and preparing feasts days in advance of Christmas, Easter, and Purísima. Holiday feasts are shared with friends and family, and sometimes the diners can number in the hundreds. Some of the special foods usually reserved for holiday meals are *chicharrón* (chee-chahr-ROHN, or fried pork skins) and *vigorón* (bee-gohr-OHN, or *chicharrón* served on a bed of raw shredded cabbage and cooked sliced yucca). An especially prized dish is *bajo* (BAH-hoh), a hearty beef or pork stew made with many indigenous vegetables and tubers.

A holiday feast would not be complete without sweets. Easter season brings *buñuelos* (boo-nyu-EH-los), fried dough made of cassava, white cheese and egg, topped with hot sugar syrup. For Christmas, women prepare *almivar* (al-me-VAHR), a grated candied fruit. Purísma specialties include a crumbly bar made of ground corn, ginger, and sugar, called *alfajor* (al-fa-HOR), plus *ayote en miel* (a-YOT-te en me-EL), which is squash cooked in honey, and light, crispy *espumillas* (es-pum-EE-yahs) or meringues. Children would go door to door for sweets, such as caramel and chopped sugar cane.

KITCHENS

Aside from the living room, the kitchen is the most often used room in a typical middle- or lower-class home. It is where families eat because small houses do not have separate dining rooms. Women wash clothes and bathe babies in the kitchen sink or in a large wash basin kept outdoors. A radio is almost always found in the kitchen because Nicaraguans love to listen to music. Usually the kitchen table is the only table in the house, so children often do their homework there. Upper-class families have dining rooms where meals are usually served. They can also afford to hire maids to cook and clean, and the kitchen then becomes the cook's domain.

Average households might have a refrigerator or a wood stove, but not both. Neighbors often "borrow" each other's kitchens when they need to bake or keep food cold. In the mornings, coffee is brewed, not in an electric coffee maker, but in a big pot on the stove. People without stoves cook on two-burner electric hot plates.

A big frying pan is essential, and most kitchens also have several pots in various sizes, enough eating utensils and plates for each family member, as well as a few extra, and a large jug for storing boiled water for drinking. Cups and glasses are scarce, so people often drink out of cut-off soda pop bottles with the edges smoothed. A hollowed-out gourd works like a thermos cup, keeping drinks cold even without ice. Milk and juice are stored in small plastic bags that hold one or two servings. Fresh orange juice is served in its own natural cup, made by slicing off the top and carefully cutting away the skin. The spongy white part is left intact so one can hold the orange in one hand and eat it by squeezing and sucking.

Above: **Tortillas prepared on a hot wood stove are a staple item during meals.**

Opposite: **A procession celebrating Purísma on Ometepe Island.**

127

RESTAURANTS

Although the majority of Nicaraguans do not eat out very often, there are enough wealthy locals and foreigners to keep even the most expensive restaurants in business. At the Intercontinental Hotel in Managua, U.S. dollars or a credit card will buy an enormous breakfast (about $8) or an all-you-can-eat lunch (about $12). Estelí, Matagalpa, and Managua are three of the best cities for eating out—everything from seafood and steaks to Mexican and Thai food is available. There are restaurants specializing in French cuisine, European dishes, or Swiss desserts. Many Salvadorean restaurants are also found in Managua and León.

Several health food restaurants in Nicaragua have recently gained popularity; some serve only organically grown food. Fast food in Nicaragua means one of three things. The first option is eating at an outdoor stand called a *fritanga* (free-TAN-ga), where grilled chicken, beef, and pork

"ONE BIG MAC AND A SIDE OF CASSAVA, PLEASE"

Today there are three McDonald's in Managua. They serve standard McDonald's fare, cooked the standard McDonald's way. But that was not always the case.

In 1975 the franchise opened its doors to Nicaraguans who had never before seen the Golden Arches. The establishment also became popular with foreign visitors who wanted something familiar to eat. But within a few years, customers began complaining to McDonald's International (the parent company of McDonald's branches) about the quality of food served at McDonald's Managua. In 1986 the owner of the local McDonald's received a letter from headquarters that warned, "Do not sell cheeseburgers unless they contain cheese." Well, that was easier said than done in a country where even milk was in short supply. After the Sandinista revolution, supplies were limited because of the U.S. trade embargo. McDonald's Managua could not import pickles for their Big Macs or the regulation paper to wrap burgers. For a while, the restaurant used Russian wrappers, but customers complained they made the food smell (and taste) like wet cardboard.

The staff used white cheese when there was no yellow cheese, substituted cabbage for lettuce, and when they ran out of french fries, they served deep-fried cassava (a tropical plant with a starchy root that is also used to make tapioca). Coca-Cola was rarely available, so the restaurant sold *pitaya* (pee-TAH-yah), a tropical cactus-fruit drink.

While the people at McDonald's International were not pleased about these practices, they could not do much about them. To make things worse, they could not even get their profits if they closed down the restaurant because foreign exchange had been cut off. Finally, in 1988, the owner voluntarily severed ties with McDonald's International by changing his restaurant's name to Donald's.

"... a twelve-year-old boy walks by selling shelled peanuts. 'Maní, maní, maní!' Peanuts, peanuts, peanuts! There are a lot of kids who sell peanuts. They sell them on the streets, on the buses, at the bus stops to the people waiting in line, in bars at night. They buy the nuts at the beginning of the day in a giant bag, and then they repackage them into tiny plastic bags."

—*Rita Golden Gelman, Inside Nicaragua*

are served. The second, much more expensive option, found mainly in Managua, is American fast food chains such as Subway or McDonald's. These chains serve exactly the same food found at their U.S. outlets, and cost the same too, which means it can cost 10 times as much to eat at McDonald's as to eat at a *fritanga*. For a third option, Nicaragua has its own American-style fast food. Several chains serve delicious fried chicken and chicken strips, fries, and soft drinks.

GALLO PINTO (PAINTED ROOSTER)

This traditional Nicaraguan dish that is eaten daily is easy to make. If your friends think your cooking is very delicious, they should say it is *bien rico* (bee-en REE-koh). This recipe makes four servings.

1 tablespoon vegetable oil
1 small onion, finely chopped
1 clove fresh garlic, minced or
$\frac{1}{2}$ teaspoon garlic powder
1 cup cooked white rice
1 cup cooked red beans

Heat the oil in a frying pan. Add the onion and garlic, stirring until brown. Then mix in the rice and beans and cook over medium heat, stirring constantly for 5 to 10 minutes or until the oil is gone and everything is slightly crispy. Add a few drops of hot pepper sauce if you like spicy food.

ESPUMILLAS (MERINGUES)

These simple crispy meringues are probably the most popular sweet treat in Nicaragua.

Wax paper or baking parchment paper
4 egg whites
1 cup of finely granulated sugar

Preheat the oven to between 275°F and 300°F (135°C and 150°C). Place wax paper on a cookie sheet. Beat the egg whites with a mixer on low until they are foamy, then on medium for one minute, and then at high speed for about two to three minutes until the mixture is white and stiff. Then, still mixing on high speed, add in the sugar gradually. The mixture will be smooth and glossy. Drop spoonfuls of the mixture onto the paper-lined cookie sheet and place in the oven. Bake for 30 to 35 minutes until the meringues are a toasty tan color, then turn off the oven and leave the *espumillas* in the oven until cool.

HONDURAS

A **B** **C** **D**

Capital city
Major town
▲ Mountain peak

Feet	Meters
over 16,000	over 4,877
9,000–16,000	2,743–4,877
6,000–9,000	1,829–2,743
3,000–6,000	914–1,829
1,500–3,000	457–914
600–1,500	183–457
0–600	0–183

1

EL SALVADOR

Río Coco Oregovia

Río Huahua

Miskitos Cay

REGIÓN
AUTONOMISTA
ATLÁNTICO NORTE

• Puerto Cabezas

JINOTEGA   Saslaya
(6,561 ft) ▲

Río Bambana

NUEVA
SEGOVIA

Bosawas
Biosphere Reserve

Río Prinzapolca

2

MADRIZ   Coco

Central

Río Grande

ESTELÍ

Miraflor Natural
Reserve

Río Tuma

• Esteli

MATAGALPA

Gulf of Fonseca

CHINANDEGA   San Cristóbal

• Matagalpa

Laguna
de
Perlas

Río Grande

LEÓN

Highlands

REGIÓN
AUTONOMISTA
ATLÁNTICO SUR

▲ Chinandega

Momotombo

Corn Islands

Corinto • • León ▲
Cerro
Negro

▲ Lake
Managua

MANAGUA   Mombachito

▲ BOACO

Rama • Río Escondido

3

Puerto Sandino •

• Tipitapa

• El Bluff

CHONTALES

Bluefields •

Managua •

Masaya •

Venado Island

MASAYA

Diriamba •

• Granada

Río
Tepenaguasapa

Río Punta Gorda

Monkey Point

Jinotepe •

GRANADA

Lake

CARAZO

• Rivas

Nicaragua

RÍO
SAN JUAN

RIVAS

Ometepe
Island

Solentiname
Island

San Juan del Sur •

4

PACIFIC OCEAN

Río San Juan

Indio-Maíz
Biological
Reserve

• San Juan del Norte

CARIBBEAN SEA

Mosquito Coast

COSTA RICA

5

N

PANAMA

MAP OF NICARAGUA

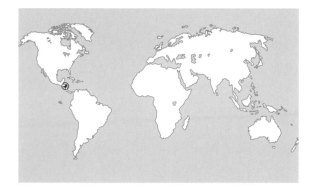

ECONOMIC NICARAGUA

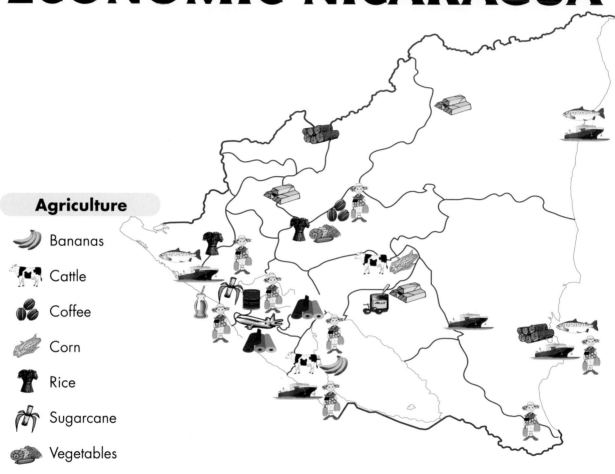

Agriculture

-  Bananas
- Cattle
- Coffee
- Corn
- Rice
- Sugarcane
- Vegetables

Natural Resources

- Fishery
- Forestry
- Gold Mine
- Petroleum Refinery

Manufacturing

- Beverage processing
- Food processing
- Textiles

Services

- Airport
- Port
- Tourism

ABOUT THE ECONOMY

OVERVIEW

Nicaragua's economy is slowly recovering from the disasters that occurred in the 1990s: the drastic fall in coffee prices and the effects of Hurricane Mitch. While the service sector contributes more to the country's GDP, the majority of Nicaragua's workforce are employed in the agricultural sector. Chronic problems, such as unemployment and underemployment, remain unresolved. Nicaragua is also still heavily dependent on foreign aid.

GDP

US$11.6 million

GDP SECTORS

Agriculture: 28.9 percent
Industry: 25.4 percent
Services: 45.7 percent (2003 est.)

LAND AREA

49,998 square miles (129,494 square km)

LAND USE

Arable land: 15.94 percent
Permanent crops: 1.94 percent
Other: 82.12 percent (2001)

CURRENCY

1 córdoba oro (NIO) = 100 centavos
Notes: 100, 50, 20, 10, 5, and 1
Coins: 25, 10, and 5
U.S.$1 = 16.31 Córdoba (2005)

LABOR FORCE

1.91 million (2003)

UNEMPLOYMENT RATE

22 percent plus considerable underemployment (2003 est.)

INFLATION RATE

5.3 percent (2003 est.)

EXTERNAL DEBT

US$5.833 billion (2004 est.)

AGRICULTURAL PRODUCTS

Coffee, bananas, sugarcane, cotton, rice, corn, tobacco, sesame, soy, beans, beef, veal, pork, poultry, dairy products

INDUSTRIAL PRODUCTS

Food processing, chemicals, machinery and metal products, textiles, clothing, petroleum refining and distribution, beverages, footwear, wood

MAJOR TRADE PARTNERS (IMPORTS)

United States 24.9 percent, Venezuela 9.7 percent, Costa Rica 9 percent, Mexico 8.4 percent, Guatemala 7.3 percent, El Salvador 4.9 percent, Japan 4.3 percent (2003)

MAJOR IMPORTS

Machinery and equipment, raw materials, petroleum products, consumer goods

PORTS AND HARBORS

Bluefields, Corinto, El Bluff, Puerto Cabezas, Puerto Sandino, Rama, San Juan del Sur

CULTURAL NICARAGUA

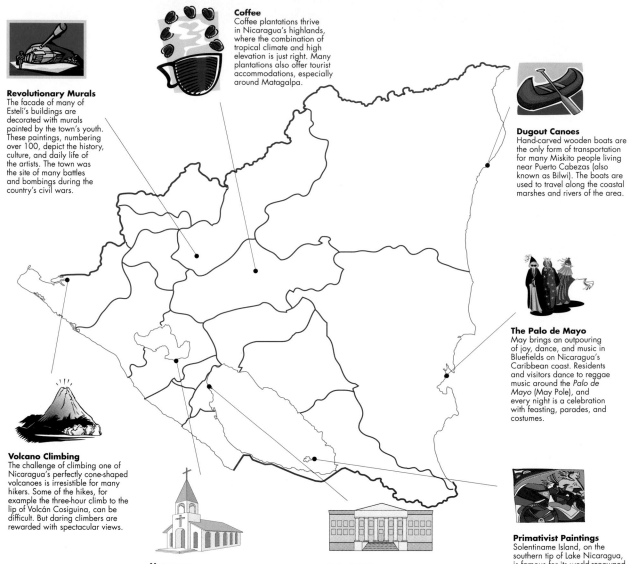

Coffee
Coffee plantations thrive in Nicaragua's highlands, where the combination of tropical climate and high elevation is just right. Many plantations also offer tourist accommodations, especially around Matagalpa.

Revolutionary Murals
The facade of many of Estelí's buildings are decorated with murals painted by the town's youth. These paintings, numbering over 100, depict the history, culture, and daily life of the artists. The town was the site of many battles and bombings during the country's civil wars.

Dugout Canoes
Hand-carved wooden boats are the only form of transportation for many Miskito people living near Puerto Cabezas (also known as Bilwi). The boats are used to travel along the coastal marshes and rivers of the area.

The Palo de Mayo
May brings an outpouring of joy, dance, and music in Bluefields on Nicaragua's Caribbean coast. Residents and visitors dance to reggae music around the *Palo de Mayo* (May Pole), and every night is a celebration with feasting, parades, and costumes.

Volcano Climbing
The challenge of climbing one of Nicaragua's perfectly cone-shaped volcanoes is irresistible for many hikers. Some of the hikes, for example the three-hour climb to the lip of Volcán Cosigüina, can be difficult. But daring climbers are rewarded with spectacular views.

Primativist Paintings
Solentiname Island, on the southern tip of Lake Nicaragua, is famous for its world-renowned, colorful art filled with strong patterns. The tradition of painting started in 1966, when a priest encouraged local jícaro cup carvers (who decorated drinking cups made from a gourd-like plant) to put their pictures on canvas.

Managua
Managua's two cathedrals are a study in contrast, one symbolizing the past and the other hope for the future. The historic Cathedral Santiago de los Caballeros stands in dignified ruins, irreparably damaged by the 1972 earthquake, while the new Cathedral de la Inmaculada Concepcion de Maria showcases modern architecture.

Colonial City
Granada was founded in 1523 by the Spaniards. The Antiguo Convento San Francisco, built by Franciscan monks in 1529, is one of the main attractions. It now houses both a beautiful church and an extensive museum, displaying, among other things, 30 pre-Columbian stone carvings that were found on a nearby island.

ABOUT
THE CULTURE

OFFICIAL NAME
Republic of Nicaragua

NATIONAL FLAG
Three equal horizontal bands of blue, white, and blue, with the national coat of arms in the center: a triangle encircled by the words Republica de Nicaragua and America Central.

NATIONAL ANTHEM
Salve a tí, Nicaragua (Hail to thee, Nicaragua) was officially adopted on August 25, 1971. Salomon Ibarra Mayorga wrote the lyrics and Luis A. Delgadillo arranged the music.

PROVINCES AND TERRITORIES
Fifteen departments: Boaco, Carazo, Chinandega, Chontales, Estelí, Granada, Jinotega, León, Madriz, Managua, Masaya, Matagalpa, Nueva Segovia, Río San Juan, Rivas. Two autonomous regions: Atlantico Norte and Atlantico Sur.

CAPITAL
Managua

OTHER MAJOR CITIES
León, Chinandega, Granada, Masaya, Matagalpa, Estelí, and Jinotepe.

POPULATION
5,359,759 (July 2004 est.)

ETHNIC GROUPS
Mestizo 69 percent, white 17 percent, black 9 percent, Amerindian 5 percent

RELIGION
Roman Catholic 85 percent, Protestant 15 percent

LANGUAGES
Spanish (official), English, and indigenous languages on Caribbean coast

LITERACY RATE
67.5 percent

INTERNET USERS
90,000 (2002)

IMPORTANT HOLIDAYS AND ANNIVERSARIES
Easter (March/April), Independence Day (September 15), Purísma (December 7), Christmas (December 25)

LEADERS IN POLITICS
Anastasio Somoza Debayle—president and dictator (1967–79)
Daniel Ortega—president (1984–90) and leader of FSLN (1984–present)
Violeta Barrios de Chamorro—first woman president of Nicaragua (1990–96)
Arnoldo Alemán—president (1997–2001)
Enrique Bolaños—current president (2002–06)
José Rizo Castellon—current vice president (2002–06)

TIME LINE

IN NICARAGUA	IN THE WORLD
10,000 B.C. Footprints made by humans as they flee a volcano eruption in Acahualinca.	
6,000 B.C. First known inhabitants of Nicaragua's Caribbean coast leave shell deposits.	**753 B.C.** Rome is founded. **116–17 B.C.** The Roman Empire reaches its greatest extent, under Emperor Trajan (98–17).
A.D. 500 A pre-Columbian culture carves stone monuments on Zapatera Island in Lake Nicaragua.	**A.D. 600** Height of Mayan civilization
800–1200 More pre-Columbian cultures move to the shores of Lake Nicaragua.	**1000** The Chinese perfect gunpowder and begin to use it in warfare.
1502 Christopher Columbus sails along Nicaragua's eastern coast.	
1524 Francisco Hernández de Córdoba starts the first Spanish settlement in Nicaragua.	**1530** Beginning of trans-Atlantic slave trade organized by the Portuguese in Africa.
1544 Nicaragua comes under the administration of the *audencia* of Guatemala.	**1558–1603** Reign of Elizabeth I of England **1620** Pilgrims sail the *Mayflower* to America.
1740 Mosquito Coast becomes a British dependency.	**1776** U.S. Declaration of Independence **1789–99** The French Revolution
1821 Nicaragua declares independence from Spanish rule.	
1838 Nicaragua becomes a sovereign nation.	
1856 U.S. adventurer William Walkers proclaims himself president of Nicaragua.	**1861** The U.S. Civil War begins.

IN NICARAGUA	IN THE WORLD
	1869 The Suez Canal is opened.
1911 The United States gains control over Nicaragua's finances.	**1914** World War I begins.
1937 Anastasio Somoza García become president of Nicaragua.	**1939** World War II begins.
	1945 The United States drops atomic bombs on Hiroshima and Nagasaki.
	1949 The North Atlantic Treaty Organization (NATO) is formed.
1956 Somoza is assassinated by poet Rigoberto López Pérez.	**1957** The Russians launch Sputnik.
	1966–1969 The Chinese Cultural Revolution
1967 Anastasio Somoza Debayle becomes president.	
1972 Major earthquake destroys Managua.	
1980 The FSLN wins control of the government. Contra War begins.	**1986** Nuclear power disaster at Chernobyl in Ukraine
1990 Violeta de Barrios Chamorro becomes Nicaragua's first woman president.	**1991** Break-up of the Soviet Union
1997 Arnoldo Alemán wins presidential election.	**1997** Hong Kong is returned to China.
1998 Hurricane Mitch devastates Nicaragua.	
2001 Enrique Bolaños becomes president.	**2001** Terrorists crash planes in New York, Washington, D.C., and Pennsylvania.
2003 Former president Alemán jailed for corruption.	**2003** War in Iraq

GLOSSARY

barrio
A poor neighborhood.

compadrazgo (kahm-pah-DRAHZ-goh)
Godparents, chosen by a child's parents to assist, among other things, in the child's moral upbringing.

conquistadores
Spanish conquerors who went to Central America in the 16th century.

Contra
A counter-revolutionary, someone who opposes the Sandinistas.

dictator
A ruler who assumes absolute authority.

fictive kin
People who are not really relatives but are so close that they consider each other family.

fritanga (free-TAN-ga)
An outdoor stand that sells grilled meats and other foods.

gallo pinto (GUY-oh PEEHN-toh)
A favorite dish made with white rice, red beans, and spices; the name means "painted rooster" because of the red and white colors.

guerrilla
Covert military fighter opposed to the government, or the clandestine tactics used by such a fighter.

junta
A group of people who controls the government after a revolution or coup d'état.

mestizo
Someone who has both Indian and Spanish ancestry.

nacatamale (nah-caw-ta-MAL-eh)
One of Nicaragua's traditional foods; a cornmeal tamale filled with pork, rice, potato, onion, tomato, and green pepper.

recompas (ray-KOHM-pah)
A former member of the Sandinista army who took up arms against the Chamorro government.

recontra (ray-KOHN-trah)
A Contra rebel who did not accept the ceasefire of 1990 and took up arms again.

refresco (ray-FREHS-koh)
A cool fruit drink served in a plastic bag.

remittance
A sum of money sent to a person or place; or the sending of money in payment for a transaction.

Sandinista
Follower of General Augusto César Sandino, or a member of the FSLN.

Somocista
Supporter of and person who profited from the Somoza dynasty.

FURTHER INFORMATION

BOOKS

Berman, Joshua and Randy Wood. *Moon Handbooks Nicaragua*. Emeryville, CA: Avalon Travel Publishing, 2002.

Dominguez, Adriana. *World Tour: Nicaragua*. Chicago: Heinemann-Raintree, 2003.

Leonardi, Richard. *Footprint Nicaragua Handbook*. Bath, England: Footprint Handbooks, 2002.

Morrison, Marion. *Nicaragua* (Enchantment of the World). Danbury, CT: Children's Press, 2002.

Plunkett, Hazel. *In Focus Nicaragua: A Guide to the People, Politics and Culture*. New York/Northampton, MA: Interlink Publishing Group, 2001.

Rohmer, Harriet, Octavio Chow, Morris Vidaure, and Joe Sam (illustrator). *The Invisible Hunters? Los Cazadores Invisibles: A Legend from the Miskito Indians of Nicaragua*. New York: Children's Book Press, 1993.

Rohmer, Harriet, Dorminster Wilson, and Virginia Stearns. *Mother Scorpion Country: Stories from Central America*. New York: Children's Book Press, 1987.

WEBSITES

Central Intelligence Agency World Factbook: Nicaragua.
www.cia.gov/cia/publications/factbook/geos/nu.html

Lonely Planet World Guide: Destination Nicaragua.
www.lonelyplanet.com/destinations/central_america/nicaragua/index.htm

Nicaragua Tourism Institute. www.intur.gob.ni

U.S. Aid: Nicaragua. www.usaid.org.ni

The World Bank Group (type "Nicaragua" in the search box). www.worldbank.org

MUSIC

Music From the Caribbean Coast of Nicaragua: Anthology Vol 1. Dimension Costeña.

Music From the Caribbean Coast of Nicaragua: Anthology Vol 2. Dimension Costeña.

Music from Nicaragua Libre. Rounder Select, 1992.

VIDEO/DVD

Carlos Mejía Godoy En Concierto. Mantica Waid & Co., 2001.

Globe Trekker: Central America. 555 Productions, 2003.

Hispanic Culture: The Sights and Sounds of Central America. Video Knowledge Inc., 2004.

Managua En Mi Corazón. Mantica Waid & Co. Ltd, 2000.

Tierra Mía, Nicaragua. Mantica Waid & Co. Ltd, 2001.

BIBLIOGRAPHY

Colburn, Forrest D. *My Car in Managua*. Austin, TX: University of Texas Press, 1991.

Cummins, Ronnie. *Children of the World: Nicaragua*. Milwaukee, WI: Gareth Stevens, 1990.

Gelman, Rita Golden. *Inside Nicaragua: Young People's Dreams and Fears*. New York: Franklin Watts, 1988.

Gooren, Henri. *The Religious Market in Nicaragua: the Paradoxes of Catholicism and Protestantism*. Exchange, Vol. 32 Issue 4, 2003.

Hanmer, Trudy J. Hanmer. *Nicaragua*. New York: Franklin Watts, 1986.

Kinzer, Stephen. *Blood of Brothers: Life and War in Managua*. New York: Putnam Publishing Group, 1991.

Lancaster, Roger. *Life is Hard: Machismo, Danger and the Intimacy of Power in Nicaragua*. Berkeley and Los Angeles: University of California Press, 1992.

Rushdie, Salman. *The Jaguar Smile*. New York: Picador, 2003.

Country Studies: Nicaragua. www.country-studies.com/nicaragua

Nicaragua Network. www.nicanet.org

Nicaragua Country Commercial Guide 2004. strategis.gc.ca/epic/internet/inimr-ri.nsf/en/gr126555e.html; strategis.ic.gc.ca/epic/internet/inimr-ri.nsf/en/gr126566e.html; strategis.ic.gc.ca/epic/internet/inimr-ri2.nsf/en/gr-01259e.html ·

UNICEF. www.unicef.org/infobycountry/nicaragua_24060.html

U.S. State Department: Nicaragua. www.state.gov/r/pa/ei/bgn/1850.htm

INDEX

143